# The Two Great Lights

*A Comparison of Law and Grace*

*By Joe Butler*

Joe Butler

## *What People Are Saying*

I met Joe Butler years ago when I heard a member of my church was in the emergency room. I entered a dark room and realized Joe was struggling with a serious eye affliction and really needed a touch of God. As I prayed with him and then visited, I remember thinking, "Who is this man?" I realized that this was not your normal Sunday only follower of Christ but a true disciple who had been involved in ministry, passionately pursued spiritual growth and was able to walk by faith in a difficult time. Over the years I have had the privilege of seeing he and his wife teach small groups, Sunday School classes and eventually become part of the Eldership at Cornerstone Church Nashville. His constant willingness to serve, support and seek the church's growth and health are abnormal in today's self-seeking world and a breath of refreshing to this pastor and so many others. Joe Butler is a man who has been a blessing in every way a fellow traveller could be. As I read through the book and observed the simplicity of thought yet the depth of insight, I knew this book needs to be read. To my preacher friends there are SERMONS in here! To everyone there are fresh insights into great Bible stories as well as Biblical insights that will build faith for today's challenges. Take your time, read it slowly, discuss it with a friend and share it with others.

Maury Davis

...

In a world cluttered with uncertainty, Joe Butler, within the pages of this book, brings a clarity that is so desperately needed in the church today. Too often, too many believers are told by "would-be" do-gooders that they must check a certain number of boxes to be accepted by God. It seems so contradictory in light of passages such as Romans 5:8 "But God demonstrated His own love toward us, in that while we were yet sinners, Christ died for us (NASB)." I encourage you, take the time to read this book. Read it with the intent of the author in mind; to demonstrate that God loves you and in His love for you, grace abounds.

Pastor Jim Kubic
Launchpoint Church

...

I have known Joe Butler for many years. For at least ten of them, I was privileged to be his pastor and to walk with him and his wife, Shelly, as they loved and served Jesus. It is a privilege to endorse his first book, *The Two Great Lights*. This book captures the qualities of thoroughness, consistency, and simplicity, which I have admired for years in Joe. Joe does not ask you to believe something about our loving Father based only on his word or experiences. Every proposition Joe set forth in the book is backed up by Scripture. Joe has studied his topic and has taken the time to explain that which he has learned in clear and straightforward language. I have often waded through scholarly works that seem to be written for other scholars and not for the average pastor or layperson. That is not the case in Joe's writing and teaching. His heart is for laypeople to understand clearly the truths he has explored and discovered.

Rev. Rick Glowacki
Pastor - Columbus First Assembly of God

...

Joe Butler has not only been a friend but was also a part of my traveling worship ministry for many years. During that season, I had the wonderful opportunity to walk closely with both Shelly and Joe as well as be a part of their family and we have continued our friendship over the years. As we travelled the USA and several countries, I observed Joe as a man of integrity and a man who devoted himself wholly to the love of scripture and the spreading of the Gospel. The Two Great Lights is a book that will draw you into Joe's own journey of study through the word and the two covenants of the Bible. It is evident that he has researched, prayed and sought the help of the Holy Spirit as he draws the reader into the depth of the Father heart of God. This book is like no other I have read and will awaken your heart to the simplicity of the grace and love of God. Joe has the ability to take a deep theological subject and simplify it for the average reader. Joe delights in taking a premise and backing it with scripture, stories, and examples that invite the reader to dig deeper into the beautiful grace and love of Christ. Journey with Joe and watch the scriptures open up to reveal the love of God who gave His only Son to redeem a lost and dying world.

Rev. Julaine Christensen
Writer, worshiper and evangelist –
Current Fire Ministries

...

I've known Joe and his wife Shelly for several years. They both have such a heart for the Lord.  Every time that I talk with them, they always have a smile on their face and are such a joy to be around. I've attended several classes that Joe has taught since attending Cornerstone. Joe has a passion and love for the Bible. By reading this book, you will see the passion and love that Joe has for the bible stories that reflect God's plan and purpose between the Old Testament and New Testament. I am honored to give my endorsement for *The Two Great Lights*.  Joe does a marvellous job communicating in such a way that the common person can understand and relate. He brings to life how the bible is all about Jesus - from Genesis to Revelation.

Pastor Herb Hardcastle

…

The Two Great Lights teaches us through heartfelt lessons by the author. Learn how to overcome life's storms by knowing a loving God and what a real father is. Author Joe Butler does a wonderful job as he depicts God's love through biblical teaching that highlights how God loves us no matter what we do. There is nothing that we can do through our own works to gain His love. Jesus accepts us where we are and loves us unconditionally. This book brings so many scriptures to my mind. *"How beautiful are the feet of those who preach the gospel of peace. who bring glad tidings of good things!" - Romans 10:15. "Seek the Lord while he may be found. Call upon his name. Let the wicked forsake his way, And the unrighteous man his thoughts. Let him return to the Lord, And He will have mercy on him, and to our God, For He will abundantly pardon." - Isaiah 55:6-7.*

Josie A. Butler<br>Author - When It Rings True

…

This book is one that I believe every person should read, whether you have been a Christ follower for one day or fifty years. A large part of discipleship is about empowering believers to know who they are in Christ and what power they are connected to through Him. Studying books like *The Two Great Lights* will help you not only understand the difference between the Law and Grace but discern when others are misusing the two.

Jeff Gregory<br>Founder and president - Reaching 360

…

## *Acknowledgments*

I would like to acknowledge a few people who have inspired me and instilled in me a desire to examine Scripture through research, meditation, and discussion throughout my Christian walk. Since this is my first book, I have several mentions. It is impossible to include all those who have inspired me over the years, but here are just a few.

Thanks to my wife, Shelly Butler, who has been a continuous support through the years. She has helped to solidify many of the concepts presented in this book through hours of discussion and debate.

Thanks to my children Joseph Shane Butler (we will see you again one day), Drenda Butler, Chance Butler, and Josie Butler. It was often their questions that inspired me to look even deeper in the Word for understanding.

Jim Kubic, my ministry leader and mentor who has inspired me to live life for the glory of Jesus.

Pastor Maury Davis, my long-time pastor at Cornerstone Church in Nashville, who has challenged me to be more disciplined and dedicated to the cause of Christ.

I would like to thank all the pastors I have known over the years who poured into my life. Pastor Bob who was there for us when we lost our son, Pastor Herb, Pastor Galen, Pastor Sandy, Pastor Jeff Gregory, Pastor Rick Glowalki, Pastor Randy Williams who was my first pastor after I got saved, and many more pastors too numerous to mention.

Julaine Christensen who took a young guitarist and his family on the ministry road and inspired us with her improvisational worship and message of the love of Christ.

Also, a special thanks to my Mom, Josie Butler who made sure myself and my siblings (Greg, Angie, and

Frankie) were always taken care of, and who is one of the strongest believers I know.

Thanks to all those who attended my life group sessions, Bible studies, and events over the years and for listening and commenting as I developed these concepts.

I attend a large church and just want to give a shout out to the great people of Cornerstone Church in Nashville who have been my friends, helpers, counsellors, encouragers, and so much more over the years! Brad, Bill, Ashley, Paul, Jack, John, Jeff and Debbie, Chuck, Natalie, Buck, Tony, Gail, Greg, Randy, Thomas, Ray, Dave, Clay, Rylee, and so many more that it would be impossible to name them all. So many people have made an impact on me with their stories, and their dedication to Christ. Please know that I am deeply grateful to all those who have poured (and continue to pour) into my life as well as my family's life.

## *Preface*

I gave my life to Christ one night in 1980. I simply knelt on my bed and prayed, "God I am not living right. If You are real, please come and help me. I want to know if You are real."

He certainly did show up (but that is a story for another book). His Spirit touched me that night and I soon abandoned my life of sex, drugs, and rock and roll and landed in a small Pentecostal church in Marysville, Kansas. It was there that I fell in love with the church and church people. They welcomed me into their community, long hair and everything! It was (and still is) a great feeling being a part of the family of God.

When I was saved in those early days, I knew that God loved me. I remember thinking, "If He saved me when I was such a mess, how much more does He love me now that I am trying to do good?"

But, as I went to Bible college and various churches, I found myself worrying sometimes if I was even saved. I wasn't sure why. I was not sinning (at least not like I had been before I knew Christ), yet still I was never sure if I quite lived up to God's high standards. I always felt like I fell short.

This book is about the journey from *great joy in knowing that God loved me* to *always wondering if I was good enough.* It is about returning to that great joy you had when you first got saved and living in that joy for the rest of your life, knowing that you are saved and that the blood of Jesus Christ is stronger than anything the enemy can throw at you.

I put this book together because I recognize that there are many people who have lost their joy in living and serving God and others. Although I am currently a lay minister, I have done much in the kingdom of God. I studied the Bible and played Christian rock music while I attended Central Bible College (Springfield, Missouri). I played guitar in a few Christian Bands in college and in California (New Jerusalem, Cry, and Rock Haven). I played guitar for about twelve years for Julaine Christensen (an amazing worship evangelist to the Midwest and around the world). My wife Shelly and I, along with Josie Butler (my Mom) founded Marysville Christian Fellowship, a church in Marysville, Kansas. My wife and I have resourced several churches and schools in Kenya, China, and the USA. I have been a teacher, care group leader, usher, and elder while attending Cornerstone Church in Nashville, Tennessee, for almost twenty years now.

I simply have a great love for the word of God, and I enjoy teaching. It is my prayer that this book will help shed some light on your assurance of salvation and eliminate any burn-out you may experience in serving Christ. God's people should be the happiest, most joyful, and most energetic people on the planet. These are some of the key principles I learned that gave me back the joy and energy to live a victorious life! I hope they do the same for you.

# Table of Contents

# Chapter 1
# The Two Points of View

Now I am scared. Will I make heaven? The preacher just said that God puts a curse on those who do not bear fruit.

"Jesus cursed the fig tree," he said, "and if you do not bear fruit, God will curse you."

Is that true? Am I bearing fruit? What does bear fruit even mean? Maybe I am cursed *already*. Maybe that is why I struggle. Maybe that is why my son died. My head is reeling with thoughts of inadequacy. I can't shake it. I am not certain that I qualify for eternal life.

Are we doomed to a life of uncertainty? Always wondering if we measure up to God's standard. Never sure if He is pleased with us. As soon as it feels like I am getting my life right and God is happy with me, something (or someone) comes along to take me down a notch.

"Because you are neither hot or cold," the preacher paraphrases Revelation 3:16, "He will spew you out of His mouth."

What the heck does that mean? I've heard it before, and each time, it makes me feel completely condemned. I slump down in my chair with a sense of helplessness, wondering if I fall short of the holiness that God requires of us.

This type of church service is not an anomaly. It is something that happens in sanctuaries all throughout the world. Well-meaning preachers try to motivate their congregation to "do the right thing" often through fear and intimidation (sometimes unintentionally).

Fear is a powerful motivator. It *can* be a strong incentive for some people. It can make them think twice before they do something they shouldn't. And if fear won't change them, maybe the guilt Christians often carry (from falling short of God's law) will at least make them miserable when they do something they shouldn't.

Many motivational speakers teach that fear of loss is a much greater motivator than desire for gain. Just about every book on "successful selling" teaches this kind of motivational logic: …better purchase this insurance policy or your wife and kids will be homeless if, "God forbid," something should happen to you. Yes indeed, fear is a great motivator.

Often well-meaning church leaders can unintentionally embrace this kind of logic and incorporate it into their sermon messages. Spiritual messages become tainted with the psychology of persuasion. Consequently, messages with regard to maintaining your salvation may come across harsh and condescending. If you don't measure up, (here comes the fear of loss) you would be forfeiting heaven in exchange for damnation to hell. Certainly, one would think twice before committing some sin, because the fear of hell is enough to motivate anyone to do the right thing. The gain of course would be eternity in heaven, but like many motivational speakers, most preachers don't believe that reward (heaven) is enough incentive to keep people on the straight and narrow. Many preachers purposely instill a "fear of loss" into their messages believing that it will motivate people to be holy, and certainly for some, fear can be a deterrent to bad behavior.

In the natural, fear is a great motivator. But as believers, fear (which produces guilt and condemnation) is *not* the *best* motivator. For believers, there is something that is a far superior motivator than the "fear of loss" – that being love. Love will motivate the shyest guy out of his comfort zone to muster up the courage to talk with that pretty girl who, with a single look, can cause an extreme lack of self-confidence. Love will motivate a mother or father to protect their child even if it means giving their own life to do so. Love will motivate a family man (or woman) to work their entire life to provide for their family. The love of writing will motivate an unpublished author to continue to produce book after book. Love of music will motivate a musician to continue to play, even in the streets, whether people will listen or not. Love is the most powerful motivator of all.

But I am not just talking about human love. I am talking about the love of our heavenly Father. A perfect love. A sacrificial love. A love that transcends time. A love that paid the ultimate price to restore a relationship that was severed so long ago.

Now, I am not saying anything new here. Most of us have heard that God is love, but let's face it: there are some Scripture passages that cause us to feel insecure and can give rise even to fear, condemnation, or guilt. If God is love, then why would He inspire the writers of the Bible to include verses that cause these types of emotions? Often, rather than seeking understanding, our tendency is just to ignore those difficult texts that make us afraid and try to do the best we can as we live our lives. We hope against hope that the good things we do outweigh the bad. Then, when we stand before God, maybe… just maybe… He will give us a pass. After all, we tried hard and did our best. Surely, He will accept us.

What a horrible way to live. Always wondering. Never sure. Trying to live up to the biblical standards by doing things that are pleasing to God but never sure if it is enough to measure up.

This brings to mind a terrible but vivid memory of my childhood. My Mom worked hard to take care of us kids. In those days, she worked and also went to night school to be an RN. My Dad, on the other hand, was not so motivated. He was a musician and liked to party. He didn't make much money and often didn't come home for days. He played the trumpet, and what money he made was spent on drugs.

Mom divorced my "real" dad when I was 5 years old. Mom soon married again, and this "new dad" would turn out to be even worse. His name was Tony. He started out good enough, but after he settled in, he became abusive to Mom and my brother and I. Tony's abuse escalated over the years. When I was around eight or nine, he would do something that is analogous to this spiritual insecurity syndrome that I have been describing. Tony would put a dollar bill in his left hand and hold it out as if he was going to give the dollar to me. The first time he did this, I quickly grabbed the dollar with a big smile on my face. He did this a few times and would say, "That's for being good."

Even though he had been abusive over the years, this "giving of the dollar" was an unexpected break from the craziness that Tony's presence usually brought.

I didn't know it at the time, but he was setting me up. One day, Tony held out the dollar in his hand, and as I reached to take it, he slapped me on the side of the head. He hit me so hard that it sent me sprawling across the room. My head hurt like crazy. I was bleeding a bit out of the corner of my mouth, and there was a loud ringing in my left ear. In spite of the pain, I was still able to hear what he said, "That's for being bad, and you know what you did."

I did not know what I had done to deserve a slap, and with Tony, it was best not to ask. From that moment on, I never knew if Tony was going to give me the dollar or a slap in the head. I was not allowed to ignore the game. I had to play or something worse may happen. It was an awful time in my childhood. I hated Tony. (Eventually, Mom divorced him, and I forgave him later in life but that is a story for another day.)

Some preaching today can give us a similar impression about God. We are never certain where we stand with Him. In spite of the Bible assuring us that God truly loves us, we often wonder if He is upset with us. When we do right, we think that He is happy with us and, consequently, will reward us for good behavior. But, on the other hand, when we do bad, we fear that He is angry with us and that He is going to curse us. I don't want to live like that, and I am pretty sure that no one else does either. I just can't believe that God wants us to live our lives in doubt and with such a lack of assurance. He is not an abusive Father. He is a loving Father and is only interested in restoring a right relationship that was severed long ago.

Consider the following Scripture…

> *"Come to Me, all you who labor and are heavy laden, and I will give you rest. Take My yoke upon you and learn from Me, for I am gentle and lowly in heart, and you will find rest for your souls. For My yoke is easy and My burden is light." – Matthew 11:28-30 NKJV*

What did Jesus mean when he said this? Often, the Christian walk doesn't seem easy. It doesn't always seem like a light burden. As a matter of fact, it seems hard sometimes. For a long time, I felt as though I was letting God down. On the outside, I looked like I had it all together, but on the inside, I always had a nagging feeling that I was not doing enough. My daily walk wasn't easy. It seemed hard. But here, Jesus assured us that His yoke is easy.

I desperately desired to understand the Scripture in Matthew. Surely Jesus' words about an "easy yoke" and a "light burden" were not a contradiction to the Scriptures about the fig tree (Mark 11:12-25) or the lukewarm church (Revelation 3:14-22). I wanted that easy yoke. I wanted that light burden. Honestly, it felt that in some ways, my Christian walk was more stressful than before I had received Jesus.

Thus, began my quest to understand the words written in the Bible. Such understanding comes through the Spirit of God. Human intellect will only provide a limited understanding of Scripture. However, something amazing happens when the Spirit gives insight into His Word. Spirit revelation brings with it incredible wisdom. And in that wisdom is life and life more abundantly. In that wisdom is no fear or doubt.

> *Love has been perfected among us in this: that we may have boldness in the day of judgment; because as He is, so are we in this world. There is no fear in love; but perfect love casts out fear, because fear involves torment. But he who fears has not been made perfect in love. We love Him because He first loved us. - 1 John 4:17-19 NKJV*

Little did I know that I was about to learn something that would remove that burden of inadequacy. I am going to share it with you in hopes that you too can experience the "easy yoke" and "light burden" that Jesus promises.

Inadequacy produces fear, guilt, and condemnation. It robs you of the "peace that passes all understanding." Through knowledge and wisdom, which is infused by the Holy Spirt, I would soon walk in the liberty of the finished work of Jesus Christ and never again be subject to a yoke of bondage. Fear, guilt, and condemnation are a bondage with very heavy chains and a hard taskmaster. Those kinds of chains are broken only by the power of the Spirit not the power of the mind.

> *Stand fast therefore in the liberty by which Christ has made us free, and do not be entangled again with a yoke of bondage. – Galatians 5:1 NKJV*

I believe that all Christians want to live in the freedom that Christ has provided, the true freedom that comes from knowing Him. It is not a freedom to sin, or even to do whatever I want, but freedom from guilt. Freedom from condemnation. Freedom from that constant nagging feeling that I fall short of God's standards.

I finally found that freedom. It was right in front of me the whole time. Freedom is amazing. It is immensely liberating! The freedom I am talking about is found in those wonderful, beautiful pages of Bible Scripture! Many of you have probably read through those Scriptures before but missed the meaning. It takes the Holy Spirit to reveal it to you.

Right now, pray that the Holy Spirit will give you the eyes to see and ears to hear. Pray that He will bless you with all understanding and that He will guard your heart and mind in Christ Jesus as you begin your journey toward freedom. A freedom from guilt, inadequacy, or anything that may cause you fear. It's time to live in the victory that Jesus provides. And that victory is understood through the revelation of His Word!

So, you have a choice. Do you want to live in bondage (fear) or do you want to live in freedom (love)? It really is your choice. You must decide. Which of the two is greater? Which is the greater light? Of course, it is freedom, and freedom comes from knowing the truth. As we seek truth (spiritual truth), we are set free.

*"And you shall know the truth, and the truth shall make you free." – John 8:32*

Pastor Maury Davis, who pastors Cornerstone Church in Nashville, Tennessee, always says, "It is the truth *you know* that will set you free." It is important to study the Bible personally. Don't just take someone's word for it. Get to know the Word, and you will experience a freedom unlike anything you have ever experienced before.

I have been a Christian since I was twenty-one years old, and the Christian journey, for me, has been awesome. I am an elder at Cornerstone Church in Nashville. I started in the music ministry in 1984 and served in that ministry until 2002. I currently host a life group and have taught several classes at Cornerstone Church. I continue to serve as an elder there. I am by no means a theologian or scholar, but I do love the Word of God and believe that it contains the words of life.

I truly believe that God wants us to think of life and not death. He wants us to live in victory and not defeat. He wants us to be a bright light shining in the darkness of this crazy world. I believe that God has directed me to write this book to give light, hope, and life to my brothers and sisters in Christ and to those who do not yet know Jesus Christ.

Jesus told us that He is the way, the truth, and the life. When you seek Him, you are seeking truth and wisdom. I sincerely hope this book inspires you to fall in love with the Word of God and to seek Spirit-inspired understanding.

I pray that the next few chapters of this book will open eyes to see that Jesus is the subject of the entire Bible. Every book. Every chapter. Every verse. Even, every word! Seeing Jesus throughout Scripture will solidify a strong relationship with your heavenly Father that is healthy, joyful, exciting, and liberating!

# Joe Butler

*Therefore if the Son makes you free, you shall be free indeed. - John 8:36*

# Chapter 2
# The Two Ways to Read

In this book, I am going to show how Scripture consistently presents a picture of two covenants, i.e. the Old Testament and the New Testament, and how one is greater than the other. One is man's desperate attempt to become righteous through self-discipline and shear will. The other is living in the righteousness of the only One who had that self-discipline and shear will. One is laborious and the other is victorious! We want to live in the victory that was won through Jesus Christ, therefore we need to recognize that there are two ways to read the Bible and to gain understanding of these two great testaments.

Scripture repeatedly reveals attributes of these two covenants to its readers. They are illustrated throughout Scripture as comparison and contrast between two persons, places, or things. In each instance, one is considered greater than the other. It can be in the story of two brothers (i.e. Jacob and Esau, Ishmael and Isaac, etc.), or two trees (the two trees in the garden), or two redeemers (Boaz and the close relative), or two types of wine skins (new and old), or two wives (Sarah and Hagar). The list goes on and on. Each of these stories represents an analogy of the two covenants in one way or another, and we are going to take a very close look at some of them. But, before we begin, I want to share an important principle of Bible reading with you.

As a precursor to our journey through *The Two Great Lights,* I am going to present a wise "rule of interpretation" for gaining a deeper understanding of the Scriptures and who God is. Read this chapter very carefully, as this principle is an essential discipline for achieving insight and understanding of Scripture. It is a fundamental precept I wish I had known a long time ago.

The impartation of said principle happened to me casually, but it was the most profound wisdom I had ever acquired. It is the single best "rule" to use regarding interpretation and understanding of difficult Scripture passages. Even Bible college did not provide me with such wisdom as I am about to share with you.

It was given to me by a very wise woman who loves to talk about the Word. Since the day I met her (it was 1985 I believe) almost all of our conversations have been about the Word. The church would call her a lay person, but I have known church staff members who spend less time in the Bible than this woman. She passed this tidbit of information on to me in a conversation we were having one day, and it changed my life. I am sure it will do the same for you.

This woman is my Mother-in-Law, Pat Mataya. Pat cannot help but talk about the Bible and what she has learned; the Word of God is her favorite topic. If she is talking, it is always about the Word, or some newfound understanding, or some insight into a passage. If she is not talking about the Bible, she is talking about a book that was written by some Christian author who is discussing some topic in the Bible.

For some people, this constant sharing of the Word is irritating. One time, Pat's daughter (my sister-in-law) had to drive her from Knoxville, Tennessee to Minco, Oklahoma, a fourteen-hour drive all on Interstate 40. As

Pat shared her Biblical insights along the way, each hour of the drive became more and more intolerable for Pat's daughter. Finally, she couldn't take it anymore. She told her Mom that if she didn't stop talking about the Bible, she was going to play a Metallica CD and turn the volume all the way up as loud as it would go. Pat did stop talking, at least for a while.

Personally, I love listening to Pat talk about Scripture. It is often hard to get a word in edgewise, but over the years, as I have grown in my understanding of the Bible, our conversations have become more and more meaningful.

Even though Pat has never been on TV (she loves TBN and Christian Television) or in the limelight, her conversations carry a lot of weight. Pat Mataya is an avid reader, prayer warrior, and diligent student of the Bible.

Not only is Pat an awesome lay scholar of the Word, she also puts her faith into action. She has won thousands of people to Jesus Christ. For years, she has been going to the rough areas of Oklahoma City witnessing to street people, week after week, year after year. She has prayed with thousands of homeless people, drug addicts, prostitutes, and others to receive Christ. So, when she speaks about the Word, I listen (at least most of the time. She can really ramble sometimes). Her words carry a lot of weight with me, and I greatly value her opinion.

I gave a brief history of Pat so you can understand where this wisdom comes from and why I take it so seriously. Of all the things she has taught me and all the things she has said, there is one phrase that has stayed with me over the years.

One day, as she was sharing the Word with me, she casually said something I have never forgotten.

She said, *"If a Bible passage makes you feel condemned or scared, you are not reading it right."*

She has said that many times over the years, but it took several conversations before I caught it. The first few times she said it, the words just drifted off. They were carried away by the torrent of insight that was flowing out of her. It didn't really register with me right away. They were just words among thousands of others. I heard them, but they didn't stick.

*"If a Bible passage makes you feel condemned or scared, you are not reading it right."*

One day, while searching Scripture, pondering and meditating on some difficult verses, trying to understand what God was saying in His Word, her statement finally took root. If a Scripture verse made me feel condemned or fearful, I would pray and ask God to help me understand. I would pray, "God, this verse really scares me. I don't think I am reading it right. Can you help me?" And the more I did this, the more I was encouraged. God began to reveal His Word more and more! Slowly but surely, I began to realize that God truly loved me and only wanted the best for me. His Word was there to present the truth of His love to humanity.

You must grab hold of this "rule of interpretation" too. Treasure it in your soul now and forever! Those few words that Pat shared with me will change your life, your attitude, and your disposition! The Bible is not a book of condemnation and guilt. It is a book of victory! It is not a book of curses but a book of promises! It is not a book of punishment but a book of love! It is not a book of anxiety but a book of peace! Don't read the Bible from a foundation of fear, but rather from a solid foundation that it is good news and that God has revealed Himself to us so we can experience victory!

*For God has not given us a spirit of fear, but of power and of love and of a sound mind. - 2 Timothy 1:7*

We have been told that the Bible is an instruction manual, and, in a way, it is. However, I really hate that analogy because the Bible is so much more! I have heard this poor analogy many times from many believers. They say, "If you want to know how to live right, you need to read the instruction manual." How many people like to read instruction manuals? I don't think there is a person alive that enjoys reading instruction manuals.

Although we can gain instruction from the Bible, it is not an instruction manual. The Bible is a biography! It is a beautiful, wonderful, exciting, and amazing biography about Jesus Christ! It is actually an autobiography written by a ghost writer: The Holy Ghost! From Genesis to Revelation, the Bible is a true and accurate picture of the richest, most powerful, most loving being that has always been and will always be. It is a true and accurate composition about Jesus Christ. It certainly is much, much more than an instruction manual.

Stop reading the Bible strictly introspectively. Start reading it in light of who Jesus is. Stop trying to "fix" yourself. Immerse yourself in who Jesus is, and He will "fix" you effortlessly as you are transformed by the renewing of your mind.

The Bible is a book about a Father whose children lost their way, but He will do anything - even sacrifice His Own Son - to restore that lost relationship. If a verse makes you feel condemned or scared, you are probably not reading it right! If you are reading it introspectively, that is not wrong, but a better way (the greater light) is to read it like a biography of Jesus. Once this is in your Spirit, reading the Bible and listening to sermons is going to be an even more enjoyable and rewarding experience!

# Chapter 3
# The Two Covenants

### *The Context*

I gave my life to Jesus when I was 21 years old. Before that time, I was a drinker and a drug user. It was the late seventies - early eighties, so I was hanging around hippie type people. Suffice it to say, the group of people that I was influenced by were not highly educated. They could tell you about any kind of drug and what kind of reaction to expect. They knew all the various flavors of pot and their varying effects on the human body. They knew just about every rock band and the names of each band member in each rock band. They could quote all the words to many popular songs, but when it came to higher learning, or spiritual understanding, they just fell short.

It was at that time (late 70's), I gave my life to Jesus (that is a story for another day) and soon started attending a local Bible study. I also started visiting a full gospel church. This is where it came to my attention that my vocabulary was limited to that of druggies, hippies, and long hairs. I had to get used to new "church" terminology. I remember that if someone said the word "covenant," I thought about a room full of nuns. So, I am not going to assume that everyone knows what that word means, so here is the actual definition of covenant:

A covenant is a pact or agreement between two or more parties. Covenant is from the Latin *"convenire,"* which means come together. It is used in Scripture when God makes a commitment with humanity. It as a translation of Latin word *"testamentum,"* which means a will or testament. The definition of testament is:

1. Law. (a) will, especially one that relates to the disposition of one's personal property. (b) Will
2. either of the two major portions of the Bible: the Mosaic or old covenant or dispensation, or the Christian or new covenant or dispensation.
3. (initial capital letter) the New Testament, as distinct from the Old Testament.
4. (initial capital letter) a copy of the New Testament.
5. a covenant, especially between God and humans. (Dictionary.com, 1995)

As you can see, the words testament and covenant are often used interchangeably. They are synonyms. So, when referring to covenants, the Old Testament (OT) refers to the writings of Moses and other OT authors who give us the covenant of law. The New Testament (NT) refers to Jesus and His teachings as relayed through Paul and other NT authors who give us the new covenant, and it is often referred to as the covenant of grace.

As Christians, it is essential to have a clear understanding of the two covenants. We need to examine how the writers (who were inspired by the Holy Spirit) depicted those covenants throughout the various books of the Bible. We gain insight into the covenants by interpreting each of them within the context of the whole Bible. Often the Bible reveals hidden wisdom concerning the two covenants using historical narrative, factual stories, parables, and analogies throughout the Old Testament.

Also, Jesus often spoke about the two covenants in a similar manner (i.e. parables, stories, etc.). Paul and the other writers of the New Testament also provide excellent insight into the truths of the two covenants.

It is important that we understand both covenants and what they mean in light of their context in Scripture. This is the key to understanding the Bible and developing sound doctrine. As you read, you should ask yourself context questions. Who is this written to? What is the narrative? When was it written? What does the verse before and after a passage say? What does the chapter say? What does the book say? What does the entire Bible say? Good interpretation comes from understanding context.

Have you ever had a friend who is a collector? Maybe they collect comic books, or action figures, or movie memorabilia. Usually non-collectors think that collectors are strange (and maybe they are). Collectors, however, *"get"* what they are collecting. Usually their collecting passion started because they had some sort of emotional experience in conjunction with the items they like to collect. Take this scenario for instance.

Suppose you (a non-collector) go to a person's (an avid collector) house, and they show you an old comic book. You can appreciate it, but you are not really sure what you are looking at or even understand why that person holds it in such reverence. It is just a comic book.

The collector explains, "This is a 1963 Amazing Fantasy, issue number fifteen."

You think, "That's interesting. 1963. Seems old."

He continues, "It is the first appearance of Spider-Man."

You might say, "OK, cool. I like Spider-Man"

Now stop for a minute. Spider-Man. Just the fact that you know about the character should tell you something. You recognize that character even though you don't collect comics. Why do you know that character? You have seen him in the movies. You have seen him on cereal boxes. Spider-Man is practically known by the whole world. You just never really thought about why or what you know; you just know because Spider-Man is so common. This is how most of us approach things - even spiritual things: casually, without thought, trusting what you have heard or seen without really taking the time to learn about it. That is not good (when it comes to Bible understanding). But let's continue with the story.

Collectors love to talk about their collection, so your friend continues, "This Spider-Man story was written by Stan Lee. Though he was young at the time, it was to be his final comic book story. He never really wanted to be a comic book writer. He wanted to write great novels. Writing comics was just a starting point. Comic book writing, at that time, was all about characters who were a bit older, and most characters in comics at that time had it together or had money. Back then, the superhero was almost always rich or he was always doing the right thing. Comic book heroes never made mistakes or had any 'real' problems. Stan Lee wanted to write great books about real people. He wanted to write about their successes and their struggles. He wanted to write about real life problems. He was about to quit the comic biz to pursue his dream of writing that great American novel. Stan Lee's wife suggested that before he quit, he write a comic book story just the way *he* wanted to write it. He followed her advice, and that story was in Amazing Fantasy, Issue Number fifteen featuring the *all new Amazing Spider-Man*. Peter

Parker was just a kid (something rare in comics), and because of a wrong choice, his Uncle Ben died. The rest is history. People loved that story. The reader could relate to Peter Parker (aka Spider-Man) because he had to deal with problems just like we all do. He had to deal with many issues. How is Aunt May going to make money? How can I help provide? What should I do with this power? Stan Lee was to become one of the greatest comic book creators in the world. His characters would be known all around the world. Stan Lee stayed in the profession and has created hundreds of characters that are now household names. The Amazing Fantasy number fifteen comic book set a world record price selling for 1.1 million dollars in the year 2011." (Cronin, n.d.) (ICv2, 2011)

Now you have context! You finally grasp the collector's enthusiasm and understand what that old comic book means to him (and many others). You have a well-rounded perspective. Now you know why it is so valuable. Now *you* get it too!

Just like that comic book, the two great covenants in the Bible also have a rich heritage. You need to know that heritage. It really is *your* heritage! A great price was paid so that you could know your Creator personally. The Bible is the story of your value to God, and in the pages of that great book are the mysteries of His deep love for you. When you begin to examine the Word and learn how God has interwoven His great love and redemption plan throughout it, you will understand why God places such a high value on you. When you begin to see the stories and histories and poetry and how they are all connected to a secure covenant, then the Lord God, your Creator, will become your loving Father, and you will understand the great work of His Son, Jesus Christ! You will know how immensely valuable you are to Him. The two covenants must be understood in light of their context and meaning.

## *The Promises*

Contrary to popular belief, the old covenant did not start with Moses and the law. It started 400 years *before* the law. That covenant was between God and Abraham. It starts with Abraham in Genesis chapter twelve…

> *Now the Lord had said to Abram: "Get out of your country, From your family And from your father's house, To a land that I will show you. I will make you a great nation; I will bless you And make your name great; And you shall be a blessing. I will bless those who bless you, And I will curse him who curses you; And in you all the families of the earth shall be blessed." - Genesis 12: 1-3*

Here we see that God promised Abraham four things.

- He was promised land.
- He would be a great - nation (meaning he would have many children).
- He would be blessed.
- The entire world would be blessed because of him and his descendants.

God chose Abraham. Abraham did not do anything to earn such an incredible covenant relationship. He was chosen by God to be the father of a great nation and not just the father of the Jewish nation, but also to all those who are made righteous by faith in Jesus Christ (as we shall soon see).

God singled out Abraham and would weave an incredible tapestry of spiritual truth through the events in his life and the lives of his offspring. Moses and other writers documented this story in the books of the Old

Testament. The story of Abraham is both historical and pictorial. It is a beautiful picture that God masterfully painted through time, people, and events to reveal His purpose - both to the Jews and to all humankind. As you will soon learn, these promises are not just for Abraham; they are also for us today.

> *And if you are Christ's, then you are Abraham's seed, and heirs according to the promise. - Galatians 3:29*

God gave a binding promise to Abraham, but not only is that promise for Abraham and his physical descendants, it is for Christians as well. As Christians, we are Abraham's spiritual "descendants" and have access to the promises just as his blood descendants do. Galatians tells us that as believers, we are heirs according to the promise!

### *Promise 1 - Land*

God pledged four things to Abraham and his descendants. Let's look at the first promise.

> *"...To a **land** that I will show you."*

God promised Abraham that He would give him land. The very first words that God spoke to Abraham were a pledge that he would inherit a good land. This is the first mention of the promised land. It was promised to Abraham and his seed.

God would confirm His promise that He had spoken to Abraham with a covenant ritual that was common at the time. In Bible days, when two people wanted to make covenant with one another, they would take animals and cut them in half, then lay the pieces in a way in which the two covenant partners could walk between the pieces. It was called "cutting a covenant." This ritual was executed to declare to each of the covenant makers that if either would break the covenant, then the person who broke it would be torn in pieces like the dead animals they walked through. Jeremiah gives us some insight into this covenant "cutting" with the following passage…

> *And I will give the men who have transgressed My covenant, who have not performed the words of the covenant which they made before Me, when they cut the calf in two and passed between the parts of it - the princes of Judah, the princes of Jerusalem, the eunuchs, the priests, and all the people of the land who passed between the parts of the calf - I will give them into the hand of their enemies and into the hand of those who seek their life. Their dead bodies shall be for meat for the birds of the heaven and the beasts of the earth. – Jeremiah 34:18 - 20*

As you can see, the covenant process was serious, and it was a bond that could not be broken without dire consequences. But the covenant God made with Abraham was even more special.

> *And it came to pass, when the sun went down and it was dark, that behold, there appeared a smoking oven and a burning torch that passed between those pieces. On the same day the Lord made a covenant with Abram, saying: "To your descendants I have given this land, from the river of Egypt to the great river, the River Euphrates— Genesis 15:17 - 18*

In the preceding passage of Scripture before verse seventeen, we learn that Abraham fell into a deep sleep. God, represented by the smoking oven and burning torch, was the only one who would walk between the pieces of dead animals. Abraham never had a chance to walk through. This is an *unconditional covenant!* God caused Abraham to fall asleep for a reason. As human beings, we often neglect our vows and end up breaking our word, our covenant. God made sure that He alone was the only one to walk between the pieces. Therefore, the covenant is based on God's commitment alone. God is righteous and just and will always keep His covenant in spite of humankinds' tendency to fail. Therefore, the covenant is always binding because God is eternal. Also, He will not break covenant as He is always faithful, and His Word is always true. The covenant was between God and Abraham. But God is the keeper of the covenant, and it is always binding as Abraham did not walk between the pieces. Only God walked through. The strength of the covenant is based only on God's ability to keep it, and He is well able.

Notice that God is represented by two symbols. He was represented by the smoking furnace and the burning torch. Many scholars believe that the smoking furnace represent the Israelites bondage in Egypt, and the burning torch represents their great deliverance from their taskmasters. I agree that this is a wonderful picture of bondage and delivery.

I also believe that each of these symbols can also represent the two covenants. The smoking furnace represents the old covenant of law, and the burning torch represents the new covenant of grace.

The smoking furnace is a picture of the law and speaks of the holiness of God. It speaks of His judgment. Because God is holy, He must judge sin. The law condemns and demands judgment on sin.

*Now Mount Sinai was completely in smoke, because the Lord descended upon it in fire. Its smoke ascended like the smoke of a furnace, and*

*the whole mountain quaked greatly. – Exodus*
*19:18*

The law demands that we live righteous lives, but we are unable to follow the law completely. That is why, when God gave the law, He also gave instructions for animal sacrifice. We must have a sacrifice to cover our sins and our inability to follow the law to His satisfaction. The smoking furnace can easily be a picture of the old covenant.

The burning torch is a picture of Christ. He is the light of the world. He is the one that delivers us from the darkness to guide and lead us into light.

*Then Jesus spoke to them again, saying, "I am*
*the light of the world. He who follows Me shall*
*not walk in darkness, but have the light of life."*
*– John 8:12*

Jesus came that we might experience the amazing grace and favor of God. This grace is made known through the sacrifice of Christ. Because Christ took our judgment, we now have the Holy Spirit living in us, and we are the righteousness of God in Jesus Christ.

*For Zion's sake I will not hold My peace, And*
*for Jerusalem's sake I will not rest, Until her*
*righteousness goes forth as brightness, And her*
*salvation as a lamp that burns. – Isaiah 62:1*

Christ is a burning lamp (torch). Christ is our salvation. Christ is our righteousness. Christ's sacrifice satisfies God's judgment and supplies righteousness through His grace! We will discuss this in more detail later.

Let's get back to the topic at hand. God promised Abraham the land. It was a special land and was reserved for Abraham and his seed. God made sure that the Jewish nation retained their land. It has been theirs since God promised it to Abraham and consummated the covenant by passing through the cut animals. Although many have tried to take Israel's land, God has preserved it through the ages. He has brought His people back to it many times, and it is a miracle of God that the Jewish nation exists in the land that was promised. The Lord God is a covenant keeping God!

Did you know that we, as Christians, are also heirs of the "promised land" as well? I'm not talking about the dirt—the physical land of Israel. Of course, the land was literal to Abraham and his physical seed, but it is also a picture of what Jesus would provide for us when we believe. We enter the *spiritual* promised land the day we accept Christ into our lives. We too are partakers of the promise to Abraham through faith in Christ. We are spiritual seed, and the spiritual inheritance is even greater than the physical inheritance.

> *For if Joshua had given them rest, then He would not afterward have spoken of another day. There remains therefore a rest for the people of God. For he who has entered His rest has himself also ceased from his works as God did from His. - Hebrews 4:8-9 NKJV*

The Bible calls the promised land God's rest. The promised land is called "His rest" because it is a land filled with milk and honey. It represents God's supply for the well-being of His people. The Bible tells us that upon entering it, the Jewish people would drink from wells they did not dig and eat from vineyards that they did not plant. They were to rest in God's provision of a great land, ripe with food and shelter. Joshua did bring the people across the Jordan River and into the land that God promised to Abraham, yet the writer of Hebrews is saying that Joshua did not bring the people into God's rest, but rather that Christ would. What does this mean?

Joshua brought the people into the land physically. He crossed over the Jorden River with them, and the Jewish people did take that land under Joshua's leadership. This is a great story that is told in the Old Testament. It is historically true, but it is also a picture of something much greater. There is an even greater promised land. There is an even greater Joshua. There is an even greater rest.

That greater Joshua is Jesus. Jesus brings us into God's rest. It is Jesus who has brought us (Christians) out of Egypt (bondage and death), through the dessert, and into the promised land (freedom and life). The day we believed in Him, we ceased to be of this earthly (temporal) kingdom and are now part of His heavenly (eternal) kingdom. We have been given the Holy Spirit as a pledge that we have entered into His rest! He is our provision. He is our vineyard. He is our milk. He is our honey. He is our dwelling place! The true promised land that the Christian enters into is greater than the physical promised land which the Jews entered 3,600 years ago!

God has provided the fulfillment of a covenant spoken to Abraham 4,000 years ago. He has fulfilled that covenant both physically (through Moses and Joshua) and spiritually (through Jesus). We, as Christians have entered that promised land of God's rest by faith in Jesus Christ.

## *Promise 2 – A Great Nation*

Now, let's look at the next pledge made in the covenant with Abraham.

*"...I will make you a great nation;"*

God promised Abraham that he would be a great nation. In order for Abraham to be a great nation he would, of course, need to have kids. At the time that God made this promise, Abraham didn't have *any* kids. Becoming a great nation would take a miracle as Abraham and his wife Sarah were unable to conceive, and they were getting old. Sarah was past child bearing years. She tried to accomplish God's promise of children through her Egyptian servant whose name was Hagar. Since Sarah couldn't have children, Sarah gave Hagar to Abraham to bear children for her. When Abraham was 86 years old, he had a son with Hagar, the servant girl, but that was not God's plan. God would later give Abraham and Sarah a son when Abraham was 100 years old, and Sarah was around 90. It was a miracle. They had the child God promised them when they were well into their years, and God would show Himself strong in their lives. They gave birth to Isaac who would then go on to produce Jacob who was later named Israel. So, the second attribute of the promise is that Abraham would be a great nation, and God brought that to pass in His timing and by a wonderful miracle.

> *And behold, the word of the Lord came to him, saying, "This one shall not be your heir, but one who will come from your own body shall be your heir." Then He brought him outside and said, "Look now toward heaven, and count the stars if you are able to number them." And He said to him, "So shall your descendants be." And he believed in the Lord, and He accounted it to him for righteousness. - Genesis 15:4-6 NKJV*

God promised Abraham that he would have so many descendants that he would not be able to number them. And God said that it would be from his own body. God was saying that He would work a miracle in both Abraham and his wife Sarah. Abraham believed God, and because of that trust in God, Abraham was given the gift of righteousness. He simply trusted God, and that faith was accounted to him for righteousness.

Through Abraham's son, Isaac, came the Jewish nation. The Jewish nation was born out of the miracle birth of Isaac! As of the date that I am writing this, the Jewish nation is currently about fourteen million people. That is only about two tenths of one percent (.002%) of the current entire population of planet earth. The Jewish people are a blessed nation. Over the years, they have survived many hardships, but they are still small *in number* compared to other nations like China, India, and the other Arab nations. So, how is it that God can say Abraham's descendants will be like the stars of heaven? Or the grains of sand in the sea?

Again, this promise extends to the believer in Christ as well. As Christians who have been "born again," we too, through a miracle birth, become part of Abraham's family. We are joint heirs, and we can consider Abraham as our "father," so to speak—even if we are not Jewish. If you are a Christian, you are a child of Abraham. He is the father of all those who are justified by faith.

> *Therefore it is of faith that it might be according to grace, so that the promise might be sure to all the seed, not only to those who are of the law, but also to those who are of the faith of Abraham, who is the father of us all (as it is written, "I have made you a father of many nations")... - Romans 4:16-17*

Romans tells us that believers who are justified by faith in Jesus Christ are considered children of Abraham. He is the father of faith, and we are his children when we exercise faith in Christ. Now, it is quite easy to see the fulfilment of the promise in which Abraham is a father to a great nation—a nation that has been given the promises of God! So, the promise that Abraham would be a father to a great nation is true even today with untold millions of Christians and Jews as his descendants both spiritually and genetically.

### *Promise 3 - Blessing*

*I will bless you And make your name great;*

God promised Abraham that He would bless him. And, just as God promised, Abraham was truly blessed. God chose him, and made his covenant with him. As he lived in that covenant, he became extremely rich. Even though Abraham was not perfect (Abraham lied about his wife to the king and to pharaoh), he was blessed and had many possessions. He had servants and livestock, and the entire world at that time knew who he was.

*Abram was very rich in livestock, in silver, and in gold. – Genesis 13:2*

These blessings continue to fall on the descendants of Abraham today. According to Steve Pease in "The Golden Age of Jewish Achievement," people of Jewish nationality have won 22 percent of all Nobel Prizes ever awarded. They have received 29 percent of the prizes since 1950 (after the Holocaust wiped out thirty-three percent of the Jewish Population). Sixty-Six percent of Broadway's longest running musicals were created by Jews. The Jews represent thirty-eight percent of directors who have earned Oscars. The comic book genius Stan Lee was Jewish. They are truly a blessed people. (Pease, 2009)

We as Christians are blessed as well. We have become joint heirs with Christ and have access to our heavenly Father. I can't speak for all Christians, but personally, I don't know that I would have survived had I not given my life to Christ. I was a drug addict and a drinker before I knew Christ. I became a Christian in 1980, and I can easily say it was the best thing that ever happened to me. I didn't make any more money, but my lifestyle changed for the better. I met better friends. I got better jobs. I was more responsible. But most of all, my life was given a purpose. I found my identity in Christ and learned who I was and where I was going. I met my Creator, and He became my Father. Being a believer gave me peace of mind—something I never had before I was a Christian.

I would imagine that most Christians, even those with limited financial resources, would say that they are better off after knowing Jesus than before. We, as Christians, truly experience the blessing of Abraham as we inherit the covenant that God promised long ago. We know that we have eternity. We are not of this world. We are of the kingdom that is to come, and there is a hope and future that will not disappoint. We are truly blessed.

### *Promise 4 – All Families Blessed*

*...And in you all the families of the earth shall be blessed.*

Society is blessed because of the Jews. Albert Einstein is a household name, and his Theory of Relativity is known by physicists as well as lay persons. Just about everyone can quote it, even though they do not know what it means. Jonas Salk created the first Polio vaccine. Selman Waksman discovered Streptomycin and coined the word "antibiotic." Because of the Jews, we have color photography, the sewing machine, denim jeans, the polio vaccine, insulin, and aspirin.

The Jews dominate the film industry. People like Samuel Goldwyn, Louis B. Mayer, and Harry Warner are recognizable as associated with film studios of the same name. Many actors like Milton Berle, Kirk Douglas, the Marx brothers, Jack Benny, Edward G. Robinson, Woody Allen, Tony Randall, William Shatner, Leonard Nimoy, Billy Crystal, Jerry Seinfeld, Dustin Hoffman, Jason Alexander, Carl Reiner, Bette Midler, and Barbara Streisand are Jewish. There are just too many to mention.

Many other contributions by Jews include the safety razor, printed circuit boards, cell phones, transistors, the computer mouse, defibrillators, video tape, the Corvette, the cotton swab, the teddy bear, Barbie dolls, and the ball point pen. (10 Great Jewish Contributions to Mankind, n.d.) (Goriss, 2016)

Truly all nations are blessed because of the Jewish people. Their contributions have touched every nation on earth. Just as the Jews have had influence on nations, Christians also bring blessing and great contributions to society. Because of this great covenant, all nations and all families are blessed. Believers and un-believers are blessed as a result of the Spirit of God on His people.

The United States prospered as people fled here for religious and political freedom over 200 years ago. We quickly became the greatest nation on earth. As a result, much of humankind has experienced, in some way, the generosity and ingenuity of the United States and its wide-reaching Christian influence.

Singapore has prospered over the last 40 years, and I believe much of that is attributed to the revival of Christianity there. Christianity has outgrown all other religions in Singapore since the 1970's, and along with that spiritual growth came prosperity. Singapore went from third world to first world country in one generation, now boasting more millionaires per capita than any other nation. (Hays, 2015)

There is convincing research that claims most nations that accept Christian evangelism experience better living conditions after accepting and allowing Christians to minister there. Because Christianity is based on the Bible, it was missionaries who taught their converts to read and write, bringing in printing presses and publishing religious literature. Missionaries were often responsible for teaching agriculture and trade, helping societies to improve their conditions (Spencer, 2017). There is also a link between missionaries and classical liberal democracy (Woodberry, 2012). The contributions made by Jews and Christians alike have vastly improved the lives of just about every nation on earth. So, the promises that God made to Abraham and his offspring are still in effect today.

## *Accessing the Covenant*

Entering into covenant with God is a great and wonderful relationship to have with the Creator of all things. It is an honor and a privilege which Abraham experienced and one that we experience today as well. When God made the covenant with Abraham, He provided a sign that would separate Abraham and his offspring as participants in the covenant. It was the act of circumcision.

> *This is My covenant which you shall keep, between Me and you and your descendants after you: Every male child among you shall be circumcised; and you shall be circumcised in the flesh of your foreskins, and it shall be a sign of the covenant between Me and you. – Genesis 17:10-11*

God commanded that Abraham and his offspring be circumcised as a sign of the covenant that God made with him. This act was something only the Jewish people would do to show themselves separate from other nations and to show that they were participants in a covenant with God.

Circumcision is an Old Testament picture or shadow of the cutting off of sin and separating yourself to God. Just as circumcision was a physical act for the Jews, we, as Christians, have a spiritual circumcision.

*In Him you were also circumcised with the circumcision made without hands, by putting off the body of the sins of the flesh, by the circumcision of Christ, - Colossians 2:11*

When you become a believer, you enter into covenant with Christ. Sin has been cut away. The Holy Spirit now dwells within you, making you a new creation in Christ. Your thoughts are different. You begin to recognize that we are eternal beings and not temporal. Your desire to live according to the convictions of the Holy Spirit begins to take precedence. You no longer live only for that which is seen in this world, but you begin to live for that which is unseen, knowing there is a spiritual world that is eternal. Your transformation is a sign to unbelievers that you are different and that you are in covenant relationship with God.

The covenant that God made with Abraham is powerful. It is far reaching. These promises have affected just about every life on earth and still continue to be part of each human beings' life even if they don't realize it.

We have discussed God's promises and how He is faithful in performing those promises in the lives of His covenant people. But what is the believer's part of the covenant? If God's part of the covenant is to provide supply, increase, blessing, and overflow, then what is our part? What do we need to do to participate in this great covenant? These are great questions. As you read on, you will see that God's covenant is accessed differently in the Old Testament than the New.

## *Law – The Old Covenant*

When people talk about the old covenant, they are often referring to the law. When you ask people what the law is, most will say the ten commandments. And, that is true; the ten commandments are part of the law. However, the Jewish tradition teaches that there are six hundred and thirteen commandments. There are laws concerning the poor, prayer, marriage, family, Gentiles, sacrifices, offerings, and many other subjects. These laws are often referred to as ceremonial laws. In the Old Testament, both judicial and ceremonial laws are to be followed if you want to be blessed by God.

In this book, we are more concerned with what the law means as well as its intent. The law reveals the holiness of God. It shows us that God desires humankind to be responsible, both to Him, and to fellow human beings. The law is a picture of who Christ is—perfect inside and out.

The Old Testament law sets a very high standard that must be followed. When someone follows the law, they are blessed. When someone does not follow the law, they are cursed. The law demands that righteousness be achieved through strict adherence of the law.

> *"Behold, I set before you today a blessing and a curse: the blessing, if you obey the commandments of the Lord your God which I command you today; and the curse, if you do not obey the commandments of the Lord your God, but turn aside from the way which I command you today, to go after other gods*

*which you have not known." – Deuteronomy 11:26-28*

There are a couple of things we need to take into consideration. Abraham was considered righteous before the law had even been given. Also, Enoch walked with God and was no more because God took him. Noah was considered a just man, perfect in his generations, long before the law came on the scene. So, if people could be considered righteous even before the law, why did God give the law?

> *What purpose then does the law serve? It was added because of transgressions, till the Seed should come to whom the promise was made; and it was appointed through angels by the hand of a mediator. – Galatians 3:19*

Galatians tells us that the law was given because of transgression. It describes how we should live and what we should and should not do. When we fall short, the law exposes our short comings. It reveals our guilt and inability to live a righteous life. The law actually condemns us because we are unable to live up to its standards. It constantly speaks of our human frailty. It was not meant to make us righteous, but rather, it was designed to bring us to the end of ourselves—to affirm that we are unable to reconcile with God through our own self-discipline. It is a measuring standard that we can never live up to no matter how hard we try.

God knew we would fall short, so He provided something that would cover our sin. Failure to live up to the standard must be punished because God is a holy God and will not allow sin to reign. Sin is detrimental to humankind, and it separates us from our Creator. Therefore, humanity is in need of a proxy, or propitiation, to take the punishment for our inability to follow the law.

Animal sacrifice began long before the law. After Adam and Eve sinned, God made them coverings of animal skin. An innocent animal had to die to cover Adam and Eve. That was the very first animal sacrifice.

When God gave the law, He also gave instructions for the various sacrifices. God knew that humankind would fall short of the law's requirements. The only way we would have recompense for sin would be through a sacrifice. The law actually magnifies sin in such a way as to make it so prevalent that we recognize our need for a sacrifice.

*What shall we say then? Is the law sin? Certainly not! On the contrary, I would not have known sin except through the law. For I would not have known covetousness unless the law had said, "You shall not covet." – Romans 7:7*

According to Romans, the law reveals our sin. It boldly proclaims our failure to achieve righteousness through clean living and trying to do good. Even if you follow the commandments perfectly in letter, Jesus made it clear that just thinking about something you shouldn't do is the same as actually doing it.

*"You have heard that it was said to those of old, 'You shall not murder, and whoever murders will be in danger of the judgment.' But I say to you that whoever is angry with his brother without a cause shall be in danger of the judgment. And whoever says to his brother, 'Raca!' shall be in danger of the council. But whoever says, 'You fool!' shall be in danger of hell fire. – Matthew 5:21-22*

Jesus said that anyone who hates his brother commits murder in their heart. Now who can live by the law? We are in desperate need of a sacrifice. In the Old Testament, the sacrifice was a lamb. In the New Testament, the sacrifice is the Lamb of God. We are in need of the sacrifice that Jesus supplied with His own perfect, sinless body.

The old covenant was accessing the blessing and promises of God through keeping the law and making animal sacrifices when someone broke the law. Over the years, the Jewish people would fall in and out of that covenant. When they served God and kept the sacrifices, God would bless them. When they served other gods and sacrificed to those other gods, there were repercussions. God would allow their enemies to overcome the Jewish people. Often, they would go into captivity because they stopped making the atoning sacrifices He had set up to cover their sins when they failed to keep the law.

This was a pattern with the Jewish people for many centuries. They would serve God and experience blessing. Then in that blessing, they would forget God, and stop serving him, and experience captivity and curse. Then they would repent and repeat the cycle again.

The Pharisees came about partly as a result of the Jewish people growing weary of being taken captive by their enemies. The Pharisaical system emerged to ensure that there was a clear understanding of the law and its meaning. Following the law completely meant that God would not judge them. The Pharisees were experts in the law and were the gate keepers to make sure the people were following it to the letter so that they would be blessed of God (Neusner, 1973).

### *Grace – The New Covenant*

So, the old covenant was a promise that God gave to Abraham, and he confirmed it with an oath. Four hundred and thirty years later, God gave the law to Moses, but the law does not annul the covenant. The promises that God made to Abraham are accessed through faith. They were never supposed to be accessed through that law. Paul talks about this in Galatians.

> *Now to Abraham and his Seed were the promises made. He does not say, "And to seeds," as of many, but as of one, "And to your Seed," who is Christ. And this I say, that the law, which was four hundred and thirty years later, cannot annul the covenant that was confirmed before by God in Christ, that it should make the promise of no effect. For if the inheritance is of the law, it is no longer of promise; but God gave it to Abraham by promise. - Galatians 3:16-18 NKJV*

So, God gave the promises to Abraham four hundred and thirty years before the law. Galatians tells us that the law could not void these promises. The law was given to reveal to humanity that we are unable to live a holy life and that we are in need of a savior. Humanity is unable to earn the right to God's promises. No matter how much we desire to follow the law, we simply fall short every time. We are unable to access the promises by keeping the law.

> *For the promise that he would be the heir of the world was not to Abraham or to his seed through the law, but through the righteousness of faith. For if those who are of the law are heirs, faith is made void and the promise made of no effect, because the law brings about wrath; for where there is no law there is no transgression. Romans 4:13-15*

The law reveals that we are sinners and in need of a savior. The law really does not keep sin from happening; rather it solidifies human error and reveals that error as sin. It actually brings an increase of sin because through the law humanity understands what God considers right and wrong.

> *Moreover the law entered that the offense might abound. But where sin abounded, grace abounded much more, so that as sin reigned in death, even so grace might reign through righteousness to eternal life through Jesus Christ our Lord. – Romans 5:20-21*

Here we learn that the law entered so that the offense might abound. It was given so that humanity would understand that we woefully fall short and deserve punishment and death. Thankfully, because of the obedience of Christ, God gave grace where there was sin.

The Bible says that the law was given as a tutor to reveal our inadequacy. We are simply unable to live a blameless life when left to our own will power to do good.

> *Therefore the law was our tutor to bring us to Christ, that we might be justified by faith. But after faith has come, we are no longer under a tutor. - Galatians 3:24-25*

Since the law is unable to supply righteousness, God must supply that righteousness. In the Old Testament, God required the Jewish people to sacrifice an animal for their sin. They had to sacrifice year after year. However, God's plan was to provide a perfect sacrifice that would end all sacrifices and allow humanity to enter into a covenant relationship simply by accepting that sacrifice. That sacrifice was Jesus Christ.

About fifteen hundred years after the law was given on Mount Sinai, Jesus comes on the scene. He comes during the time of the Pharisees. The message that Jesus brings is different than the law. His message is salvation through faith in Him. That message is the reason He was crucified. It was a powerful message and caused much division. It still does.

Christ's message of faith is really not a new message, but rather the same message that Abraham speaks to us through the chapters in Genesis. Abraham believed God, and it was accounted to him as righteousness. Jesus taught that a lost person need simply believe in Him to be saved. He came to reveal the Father to a lost and dying world, and anyone who believes that He is the Son of God and puts their trust in Him will be saved.

Jesus forgave sin and healed those who had faith. His message was not well-received by the Pharisees, but the common people embraced it. Whereas the spiritual leaders of the time put a heavy burden on the people, Jesus was preaching the message of faith. And, through that faith, humanity was justified and saved. Where the Pharisees had a message of strict Old Testament law adherence, Jesus' message was one of peace with God and that His yoke was easy, and His burden was light.

Jesus would make entering into God's covenant easy for humankind. It was by no means an easy task *for Him*, but He paid the price so that we could be with Him. He would put a *light burden* on His people. This was different from the strict law keeping that had been set up in the past. In the Old Testament, the Jews had circumcision, the law, and animal sacrifice. In the New Testament, Jesus would become our circumcision. Jesus would fulfill the law. Jesus would be the final sacrifice and end animal sacrifice for sin.

Circumcision was a sign that the Jewish people were separated from their sin and that they were a special people with a special relationship with God. This is a picture of how Christ would one day cut away our sin forever through the work on the cross.

Their adherence to the law was to be a sign for other nations to reveal that God's people were a righteous and holy people. They were to be a witness to the rest of the world that there was a God and that He was good and righteous. The law was a picture of the perfection of Christ. Christ became that witness and fulfilled the law.

The sacrifices were given because God knew that they would not be able to keep the law fully and that there must be shedding of blood for the remission of sins. Each sacrifice was a continuous shadow and picture of the work that Christ would do once and for all when He came. He was the Lamb of God that came to take away the sins of the world (John 1:29).

Jesus was the Son of God, who came as a man to show us the love of the Father for a lost world. As a man, Jesus was a Jew and practiced the law. He was the only one who fulfilled the law completely. He lived a life without sin and thus fulfilled the law. Jesus did not need a sacrifice. He was a perfect man. And, as a perfect man, He was the perfect sacrifice for humanity's sin. As God, His sacrifice would end all other sacrifices. In the New Testament, Christ is our circumcision. Christ is our fulfillment of the law, and Christ is our final sacrifice.

Jesus healed every sick person who appealed to him for restoration. He came to teach us that God was our Father and that He loved us more than we could ever understand. Jesus gave us a new covenant when He made Himself the sacrifice. What used to be accessed through circumcision, law, and sacrifice would be finalized through the work of Jesus Christ. His sacrifice would end all sacrifice. The Bible says that when we accept Jesus Christ, we are circumcised in the Spirit.

> *"For he is not a Jew who is one outwardly, nor is circumcision that which is outward in the flesh; but he is a Jew who is one inwardly; and circumcision is that of the heart, in the Spirit, not in the letter; whose praise is not from men but from God. – Romans 2:28-29*

We are no longer under law, but we have died to the old and are risen to the new. Those who accept Jesus Christ are crucified with Him, and we are risen to new life with Him as well. That is the new covenant. It is a covenant that is signed, sealed, and delivered by Jesus Christ. Now we enter into that promise, or covenant, through the finished work of Christ.

The old covenant of law required that humanity must follow its demands in order to be righteous. The new covenant of grace provides righteousness as a gift through the finished work of the cross. Humanity is unable to obtain righteousness by trying to do good through sheer will power. No matter how hard we try or how well we do, we fall short.

> *But we are all like an unclean thing, And all our righteousnesses are like filthy rags; - Isaiah 64:6*

We cannot earn our righteousness. Rather, Christ has earned it for us. He took our sin, so that we might have His righteousness. It is a great exchange and can really only be understood through spiritual revelation.

> *For He made Him who knew no sin to be sin for us, that we might become the righteousness of God in Him. – 2 Corinthians 5:21*

The new covenant is entering into the promises of God through the finished work of Christ. It is not by works. It is not by animal sacrifice, and it is not by circumcision. We have truly entered into His rest and must rely completely upon the provision that Christ has made for us.

> *And He took bread, gave thanks and broke it, and gave it to them, saying, "This is My body which is given for you; do this in remembrance*

*of Me." Likewise He also took the cup after supper, saying, "This cup is the new covenant in My blood, which is shed for you. – Luke 22:19-20*

The Bible says that the first covenant had fault, and that is why we needed a second one. The fault is in the fact that we as human beings are unable to receive the righteousness it provides because we are unable to follow its demands perfectly. The old covenant is unable to provide righteousness because human beings are unable to live up to its requirements. If we could adhere to it, there would be no need for a new (different) covenant.

*For if that first covenant had been faultless, then no place would have been sought for a second. – Hebrews 8:7*

When considering the two covenants, the new covenant is the *greater light*! Rather than demand righteousness, the new covenant supplies righteousness through the finished work of Jesus Christ. The covenant that was sealed through the finished work of the cross is a covenant where our requirement is simply that we believe in Jesus Christ. He is the keeper of the covenant.

*Not that we are sufficient of ourselves to think of anything as being from ourselves, but our sufficiency is from God, who also made us sufficient as ministers of the new covenant, not of the letter but of the Spirit; for the letter kills, but the Spirit gives life. - 2 Corinthians 3:5-6*

The new covenant is not conditional on the cutting of the flesh, or the works of the flesh, or even the sacrifice of animals. It is conditional on the circumcision of the Spirit, the finished work of Christ, and the sacrifice of Jesus a sinless man yet, fully God. There is no better covenant and no better security than the new covenant, which is binding through the finished work of the cross and our faith in Jesus Christ.

Now, let's take a look at just a few passages that reveal to the reader that indeed, God had the two covenants planned from the beginning, and that He revealed them in both the Old and New Testament. The rest of this book is dedicated to searching out Scripture to corroborate the two covenants and which one is the *Greater Light.*

# Chapter 4
# The Two Great Lights

The Bible has clear, concise dialogue concerning the promises that God has made with us. Also, there are many allegorical and historical narratives that can be understood as referring to the two covenants, and they usually portray one as being better than the other. These "shadows" and "pictures" are all throughout the Bible.

The writings in Scripture are more than allegory. They are actual non-fiction accounts of people and historical narratives that give us insight into the gospel message. If these stories truly are actual historical narrative (as I believe they are), then the Bible is an amazing and special book. These factual narratives are all throughout Scripture. They present "pictures" of spiritual truth and produce validity to the belief that the Bible is divinely inspired. Stories written in ancient time, documenting a history that will parallel events which happened thousands of years after those accounts were penned. That is amazing! Whether you believe those stories in the Bible are fact or just poetry or myths, they certainly (without doubt) are "pictures" and "shadows" that help us to see more clearly the purpose and meaning of the gospel. Ultimately, they testify to the gospel of Jesus Christ.

Let's take a look at the first chapter in Genesis. Right at the very beginning of the Bible, there is an often-overlooked verse that sets up the contrast between the Old Testament and New Testament. Let's examine it closely.

As Christians, we believe that God created everything. In the creation narrative, God's first words were...

*"Let there be light."*

God pronounced light four days before he made the sun, moon and stars. Before anything existed, there was light. Light came first. Light is the priority. There must be light before anything else can come into existence.

The first words that God spoke set up the entire purpose of Scripture! Think about that for a moment. The entire Bible is a book of light. The totality of its illuminating message is pronounced through the first words of God.

*"Let there be light."*

Not only is God getting ready to create all physical matter in the universe, He is doing something even greater! He speaks a prologue that is a precursor to the most meaningful document that will ever be compiled. God will use His creation to shape a narrative through the writings of His people, throughout various time periods, that will shine a great light to a lost and dying world. Those first words that God speaks are not written simply to bring light into the physical world, but to shine a great light into our hearts and our spirit! Revelation of God is light! Understanding who He is certainly brings light into our lives. God desires to reveal Himself to us even through this first narrative. God pronounces light upon humanity from the beginning of the Bible all the way through to its end.

You could pronounce those three words after just about every major event in the Scripture. God gave an elderly Abraham a son. Could that son be a picture of Christ? Of course, it is. Isaac, Abraham's son, was to be sacrificed, and he carried his own wood up the mountain for the fire just as Jesus carried His own cross. – *let there be light!* Joseph was rejected by his brothers but ended up being the savior of both his family and all the known world, just as Jesus was rejected by His people but became savior of all – *let there be light!* Ruth from Moab, a sworn enemy of the Jews, was redeemed by Boaz her kinsman redeemer, just as Jesus redeems both Jews and Gentiles when they accept Him – *let there be light!* A lamb was sacrificed to cover a person's sin, just as Jesus became sin and was sacrificed that we might become righteous – *let there be light!* Jesus rose from the dead that we too might also rise to new life – *let there be light!* Every word of Scripture is light to a dark world. The light is of course Jesus Christ!

> *Then Jesus spoke to them again, saying, "I am the light of the world. He who follows Me shall not walk in darkness, but have the light of life."*
> *– John 8:12*

As we move on through the creation story, we come to the fourth day where God creates the sun, moon, and stars. There is much to learn in the preceding verses before He creates the sun and moon, but since we are talking about light, it just seems fitting to reveal some interesting truths here - shed some light (so to speak).

> *Then God made two great lights: the greater light to rule the day, and the lesser light to rule the night. He made the stars also. – Genesis 1:16*

Here we see that God made two great lights. One is the sun, and the other is the moon. Of course, the greater light is the sun. It is to rule the day. The lesser light is the moon, and it is to rule the night.

Usually we just read the verse and instinctively realize that this portion of Scripture is talking about the creation of the sun and moon. We keep reading without taking the time to ponder this amazing statement. There is a much greater picture here than just a pronouncement of creation, and we need to look at it a bit more closely. Scripture tells us that the sky, and the stars and objects that are in it, display a great testimony to God's handiwork. The heavens speak to us all the time.

> *The heavens declare the glory of God; And the firmament shows His handiwork. Day unto day utters speech, And night unto night reveals knowledge. There is no speech nor language Where their voice is not heard. Their line has gone out through all the earth, And their words to the end of the world. – Psalm 19:1-4*

In Psalm 19 we learn that the heavens are "speaking" to humanity. Saved or not saved, the night sky can strike awe and wonder in anyone who looks up at it. It declares His handiwork! It speaks out about His creation in a language that everyone understands! Just as God preserved His word in Scripture, He shouts out the message of His majesty day and night each time we gaze upward.

From Earth, we observe that the sun and the moon appear to be about the same size. The sun, however, is actually four hundred times larger than the moon. Scientists estimate that around 64.3 million moons would fit inside the sun. The sun appears the same size because it is four hundred times further away than the moon. Both the sun's size and distance are multiplied proportionately by about four hundred times that of the moon. So, the moon and the sun appear to be the same size. Thus, the moon can completely cover the sun during a lunar eclipse. But, although they *appear* to be the same size, the sun is truly the greater light. (EarthSky, 2013) (Reference.com, n.d.)

The science is amazing, but that is not the purpose of this book. I am hoping to shed some "spiritual light" on the meaning of the two great lights. If you ever get a chance to study the science behind these great lights you should. I just want to give you a cursory understanding of how much greater the sun is than the moon because we are about to make a comparison.

When I first read the creation story in the Bible, I thought it was a pretty cool. God created everything, and the story was amazing. I was a new Christian, so I read it quickly. I had set out to read the entire Bible, and that was no small task. It was a big book. If I was to get through it, I needed to keep reading and reading as fast as I could.

Reading fast is not a great way to read the Bible. If all you are trying to accomplish is to get your daily reading done in record time, you are not going to absorb very much spiritual insight. A better way to read the Bible is to read it *slow*. Take in each and every word. Ponder on each phrase. Consider the context. The Bible is a "God-breathed" book, inspired of the Holy Spirit, and can only be understood through revelation of the Holy Spirit. When you read the Word of God, pray and read slow. Ask God to reveal His truth to you through those wonderful, beautiful words.

Just one more important "rule of reading" before we get into the meaning of the sun and the moon. When I was younger, I used to read the Bible with the following mindset…

"How does this apply to me?"

That is not a bad way to read the Bible. We need to be introspective and understand how we can apply the Word to our lives, how we can become better people by applying the Bible's principles to our lives. Many of us grew up with the "Life Application" Bible. It came highly recommended by many in ministry. *"How can we apply this to our lives?"* said the Bible Study Teacher. That is a great way to examine Scripture. We need to apply what we learn to our daily lives. But there is an even better way to read and understand Scripture.

Reading introspective is a good way to apply Scripture to your life, but it can sometimes cause you to read past verses like the creation of the sun and the moon because that portion of Scripture really doesn't have much of a life application. There is, however, a better and more enriching way to read that passage, and even the entire Word of God. This other way is very much like the difference between the greater light (sun) and the lesser light (moon). Just as both objects appear to be the same size, but one is larger and brighter, there is a way of reading the Bible that is brighter and can shed even more light.

When reading the Word, try coming from the following mindset...

"What does this Scripture reveal about Jesus?"

Be "Jesus" centered first! Not "self" centered. This is a much better way to read and understand the Bible. Searching for Christ in the Scripture is the greater light! When you read Scripture and search for Jesus in each word, you will have a much more rewarding and enriching experience. When you read to discern who Jesus is, rather than focusing on who you are, you will begin to see the "greater light." When you realize that *"Let There Be Light"* is in every passage of the Scripture and that the Light is Jesus you will acquire a love of the Word that surpasses anything you have experienced before. You will not be able to put it down, because now you see that the Bible is not so much about you as it is about JESUS! It is shining the light of Christ to a dark world. Let There Be Light!

You see, the Pharisees were extremely diligent to study the Word. In the past, Israel had been taken captive many times. The Jewish people were tired of being captured. The Old Testament tells many stories of how the Israelites were often defeated by their enemies when they strayed from Jehovah to serve other gods. The Pharisees evolved partly as a result of the Jewish nation wanting to understand God's precepts so that they could follow them completely. If they understood the law, and followed it, they would be right with God which would hedge against going into captivity again (Neusner, 1973). The Pharisees studied the Scripture diligently. They were going to do the law without fail and pleasing God would keep them from their enemies. They wanted to make sure that they followed the Scripture so that their land would be blessed. So that they would be blessed. Little did they know that they were looking at the lesser light. Rather than studying the Scripture and seeing who God was (The Greater Light), they focused more on the law (The Lesser Light) and who they were. They exercised self-discipline to try and follow the law. They did their best to do everything right. This was not good. Consider the following Scripture as Jesus corrected them…

*You search the Scriptures, for in them you think you have eternal life; and these are they which testify of Me. But you are not willing to come to Me that you may have life. – John 5:39*

Jesus said you search the Scriptures because you think you have eternal life, but it is the Scriptures that testify of Me! That is awesome! Jesus was saying that the Scriptures (both Old and New Testament) speak of Him. That is how the Pharisees should have been reading Scripture, and that is how we should read the Bible as well. We should be searching the Scripture for Him! Jesus is the Greater Light.

When Jesus said this, only the Old Testament writings existed. I love the Old Testament. It is full of Light! It speaks about Jesus in every word. You must search the Scriptures for Him. That is the better way to read the Scripture. Don't be like the Pharisees who were trying to figure out how to follow the law more precisely in order to be more righteous. It only made them self-centered, self-righteous, and more prideful.

As Christians we search the Scriptures to find Jesus. In Him is our salvation and our righteousness. In Him is our supply and rest. We search Scripture for Him, not for that so called "three step formula" or that "seven step plan" to gain favor with God. We *have* favor *now* because of the finished work of Christ. We just need to accept it.

Remember the story of the road to Emmaus and what happened after Jesus was resurrected? When Jesus appeared to the couple on the road to Emmaus, what did Jesus say to them?

> *And beginning at Moses and all the Prophets, He expounded to them in all the Scriptures the things concerning Himself. – Luke 24:27*

Jesus expounded to them all the things concerning Himself from Moses and through all the Prophets. The Scriptures are filled with the Light of Christ. That is how you should read the Bible. That is the mindset we should have when we read the Word. Search for Jesus because the verses speak of Him, and He will supply you with all wisdom and righteousness and understanding. Let there be Light!

The Scripture tells us that the Old Testament is filled with pictures and shadows of Christ. They are not the substance, but we can see, when we read, how each story and personality within the Bible contains pictures of who Jesus is.

> *So let no one judge you in food or in drink, or regarding a festival or a new moon or sabbaths,*

*which are a shadow of things to come, but the substance is of Christ. – Colossians 2:16*

*For the law, having a shadow of the good things to come, and not the very image of the things,...*
*- Hebrews 10:1*

Picture this movie scene. The camera is focused on a character who is looking at the ground. And, as he is looking at the ground a shadow comes into view. You don't know who the shadow belongs to. It is a long dark silhouette caused by the setting sun behind the person who is casting the shadow. As the scene plays out you watch and wonder, "Whose shadow is that?" Then the character begins to follow the shadow with his eyes. Starting at the head, he follows the shadow with a slow steady gaze moving towards its source. The tension rises as the film's soundtrack plays a suspenseful musical buildup that assures us the source of the shadow is about to be revealed. The character finally looks up to see who the shadow belongs to. Is it a bad guy? Is it a good guy? Whose shadow is this? We are finally shown the face of the character who is casting that shadow. Now we see who the shadow belongs to. We are amazed! It is a classic scene done in many movies, and it gets us every time.

It is the same with the Old Testament writings. They are the shadow. They are telling us that there is something awesome casting that shadow. As we read through the Old Testament, we get closer and closer to seeing who that shadow belongs to.

The New Testament Scriptures tell us who that shadow belongs to. It is a shadow of Jesus Christ. It is a picture of God executing His plan to restore a fractured relationship with His creation. It starts with Genesis and ends with Revelation. The Old Testament writings are shadows of Christ. They are not the substance, but they speak of Him! The New Testament is the substance! It is what is casting the shadow (so to speak). Both the Old Testament (shadow) and the New Testament (substance), speak of Jesus!

Now, with these truths in mind we can move forward with the intent of this book: to reveal the difference between the two covenants through the various pictures and shadows provided to us throughout the Bible and to grab hold of the victory that is in the greater light!

Right now, we are trying to gain insight into this passage of Scripture about creation, so we are reading slow (so to speak).

> *"Then God made two great lights: the greater light to rule the day, and the lesser light to rule the night. He made the stars also." – Genesis 1:16*

We know that the two great lights are the sun and moon but stop for a moment. Let's ponder on what the sun and the moon represent. Is this just a casual reference to our closest star and an orbiting rock? Could it mean something more than just a reference to the sun and the moon? You bet it can.

We know that the greater light is the sun, and it rules the day. The lesser light is the moon, and it rules the night. But, these two lights represent something else. Every word in Scripture is important and worth contemplating. God did not mention these two astrological bodies just for posterity. Everything in Scripture means something. Every name. Every number. Every word. They all have meaning.

So, one is the greater light, and one is the lesser light. I submit to you that it could very well be that these two lights represent the two covenants. One represents the New Testament, and one represents the Old Testament. Of course, the sun represents the New Testament (or new covenant), which is the greater light that rules the day!

The moon represents the Old Testament (or old covenant), which is the lesser light that rules the night. You could say that the sun represents grace (Christ or the New Testament), and the moon represents law (Moses or the Old Testament).

> *But to you who fear My name The Sun of Righteousness shall arise With healing in His wings; ... - Malachi 4:2 NKJV*

Some scientists say that the sun is a giant fusion generator (Julia Layton & Craig Freudenrich, 2000). Other scientists believe the sun could be electrical in nature (Thornhill, 2010). Either way, the sun produces its own light and heat. All of the planets in our solar system orbit the sun. The planets receive their light from the sun, and at night we see those distant planets reflecting the sun, looking very much like wandering stars.

In Malachi, Jesus is referred to as the Sun of Righteousness! Not Son, but Sun! Very interesting. We see this picture again in the Psalms...

> *For the LORD God is a sun and shield; The LORD will give grace and glory; No good thing will He withhold From those who walk uprightly. - Psalms 84:11NKJV*

Here again, we see that God is a sun and a shield! He is our protection (shield) and our sustainer (sun). The sun is a picture of Christ. Just as the sun provides light to many objects in our solar system (including the moon), Jesus illuminates all of us. He is true light! He shines brightest of all and sheds light upon the entire world!

The moon is a representation of the Old Covenant. The moon does not produce its own light. It only *reflects* the greater light. It reflects sunlight, which bounces off the moon and is reflected back to the earth. The lesser light is only a reflection of the greater light!

Like the moon, the Old Testament is a reflection of Christ who is to come. The Old Testament does bring light into the world, but it is not a source of that light. Its illumination is not as bright as what it is reflecting. The New Covenant of Christ is the bright light. Jesus is the source. He is the substance. Just as the moon reflects the light of the sun, the Old Testament reflects the person of Christ. Of course, the sun is the greater light and is the better of the two lights. Grace (the New Covenant) is a greater revelation and a better covenant than the covenant of the law! The Old Testament reflects the bright light of the New Testament!

*The heavens declare the glory of God; And the firmament shows His handiwork. Day unto day utters speech, And night unto night reveals knowledge. There is no speech nor language Where their voice is not heard. Their line has gone out through all the earth, And their words to the end of the world. In them He has set a tabernacle for the sun, Which is like a bridegroom coming out of his chamber, And rejoices like a strong man to run its race. Its rising is from one end of heaven, And its circuit to the other end; And there is nothing hidden from its heat. – Psalm 19:1-6 NKJV*

Do you see what the Psalmist says here? He says that the sun, moon, and stars - all of God's creation - speak of His handiwork. The sun is a picture of Jesus Christ. Nothing is hidden from Him. He is the bridegroom coming out of His chamber! There is nothing hidden from Him! The heavens are telling us about God, and the heavens speak a language that anyone can understand. Every nation and race can hear the heavens declaring the glory of God if they would just listen with their heart as they ponder upon the wonders of our solar system and the universe.

*He had in His right hand seven stars out of His mouth went a sharp two-edged sword, and His countenance was like the sun shining in its strength. - Revelation 1:16*

Scripture often compares the light of Christ with the light of the sun. It certainly appears that the reference to the "Greater Light" and the "Lessor Light" in chapter one of Genesis are more than just an initial interpretation as referring to the sun and the moon. Those two seemingly inconsequential references are also pictures that declare the glory of Jesus Christ and speak clearly of the two covenants.

Notice that the night produces knowledge. In the Old Testament, we have the shadow but not the substance. We have the knowledge of Christ but not Christ. We have his law but not His righteousness. Christ is hidden throughout all of the Old Testament Scripture in shadows and pictures. But if we look closely, we can find Him.

The night (Old Testament) brings knowledge, but the heavens are a tabernacle for the sun (the Sun of Righteousness)! In the morning, the Bridegroom springs forth from this knowledge and shines brightly throughout all the day! He rejoices like a strong man to run His race! His race is to bring light to the entire world! The sun is a beautiful picture of Christ and the New Testament. The moon is a picture of law and the Old Testament, which only reflect that glory.

All of the trees and plants that God created need the sunlight to survive. They convert sunlight into food. They are unable to make food from the moonlight. Plants and trees use sunlight to convert carbon dioxide into food. This is called photosynthesis. The by-product is oxygen. At night, many plants fold their leaves, then open them up during the day to receive the sunlight. They are unable to photosynthesize without the sunlight.

Just as the trees and plants get their strength from the sun, the New Covenant is the strength of our salvation. Only the light of the New Covenant can produce life. The Old Covenant is unable to produce life. It is only a reflection. We must partake of the light of Jesus Christ and receive His Spirit to experience true life.

The Bible also explains how we are children of the day, that we see much clearer when there is a brighter light. This fact is a theme we see in often in Scripture…

*You are all sons of light and sons of the day. We are not of the night nor of darkness. – 1 Thessalonians 5:5*

As Christians, we are of the greater light. We are children of the day, and it is the greater light that governs the day! It is the light of Christ that governs those who believe in Him. As you read on in Thessalonians, the writer says that the night is for those who sleep. It is also for those who get drunk. We are not children of the night (the lesser light), but rather, we are children of the day. We are awake, and our path is well lit with the glory of Christ in us.

*For you were once darkness, but now you are light in the Lord. Walk as children of light – Ephesians 5:8*

In Genesis chapter one, it appears that God has given us a glimpse of His purpose and plan that will span over thousands of years and throughout the rest of the Bible in a single verse. There is a lesser light and a greater light. The lesser light (law) ruled for many years, but it was unable to make humanity righteous. Jesus came and brought us the greater light (grace) and took on our failings and sin so that we might be clothed in His righteousness. I see two covenants here, and, as Christians, we are ministers of the better covenant!

> *But now He has obtained a more excellent ministry, inasmuch as He is also Mediator of a better covenant, which was established on better                    promises.*
> *– Hebrews 8:6*

The New Covenant is a better covenant. It is established on better promises. The New Covenant is something that the prophets and priests of old looked forward to. They were servants, but we are sons and daughters of God the Father. They had the Spirit upon them, but we have the Spirit living in us. They had the law of God, but we have the grace and mercy of God. We have the greater light.

> *who also made us sufficient as ministers of the new covenant, not of the letter but of the Spirit; for the letter kills, but the Spirit gives life.*
> *– II Corinthians 3:6*

The better covenant is the covenant that was provided by Jesus. He is the greater light. Everything else is but a reflection of His light. In the first few verses of Genesis, God provides a great picture of the two covenants and how they will be represented (i.e. a greater light and a lesser light). As we read through some of these historical narratives and stories, you are going to be amazed at how God has woven a wonderful picture of the gospel and the two covenants all throughout His Word.

# Chapter 5
# The Two Trees in the Garden

*And out of the ground the LORD God made every tree grow that is pleasant to the sight and good for food. The tree of life was also in the midst of the garden, and the tree of the knowledge of good and evil. "...but of the tree of the knowledge of good and evil you shall not eat, for in the day that you eat of it you shall surely die." - Genesis 2:9, 17*

Choice. The fork in the road. The ability to analyze information and select a path of action based on that analysis. It may be a wise choice. It may be a foolish choice. It may be a sacrificial choice. It may be one of a hundred or more different types of choices, but it is *our* choice. We make choices every day. And we must live by them.

Humans make rational choices that involve abstract thinking. That is what set us apart from all other creatures. Rational choice is a God-given gift, and it has been our defining characteristic from the beginning. We are not animals that operate on instinct. We do have instinct, but we also have much more. We are humankind, and there is no created being quite like us.

It is said, "Life is a sum of all your choices." While that is profound and true (at least to some extent), we must not leave the human origin out of the picture. We are created in the image of God who then breathed His Spirit into our body, and we became a living soul. A living soul with the ability to choose—just like our Creator. So really, we are much more than just what our choices say about us. We are created beings stamped with the image of God. Despite our good or bad choices, we cannot escape our God-given heritage. We are made in the image of God, and we are living beings through the power of the Holy Spirt that was breathed upon us.

Although we are more than just the sum of our choices, it is still imperative that we make our decisions using the wisdom of the Spirit that God has placed within us. We acquire that wisdom through study and reading of God's Word.

The Bible was given to us by the inspiration of the same Spirit that was breathed into humankind. Each book of the Bible is filled with people who made choices— some good, some bad. The Bible is a book that provides us with insight that we can use to help us make good choices. It inspires us to attempt to make the *right* choice when we are given various circumstances. It reveals to us the tragedy that wrong choices can bring and the incredible satisfaction that comes from a right choice.

The story of the two trees in the garden of Eden is a narrative about humankind's first choice. When we are presented with a choice (like Adam with the two trees in the garden of Eden), it is in our best interest to choose wisely. We need to make the right choice or there could be adverse consequences. Unfortunately, Adam did not choose wisely, and all of humankind has suffered the consequences. Therefore, it would be wise to learn from Scripture and develop our ability to make right choices.

As adult human beings we make about thirty-five thousand choices each day (Homans, 2015)! If there is any truth in the statement that life is the sum of our choices, then we must choose wisely. In our daily lives, with each choice that we make, we need to always choose the "Tree of Life."

> *...I have set before you life and death, blessing and cursing; therefore choose life, that both you and your descendants may live; - Deuteronomy 30:19*

God made thousands of trees in the creation story. All the trees were made and bore fruit so that they could bring forth seed and multiply. There were oak trees, walnut trees, magnolia trees, and many thousands of other trees. Experts are not sure exactly how many types of trees there are. The number ranges from 23,000 to 100,000 different types of trees in the world today. (Evans, n.d.) But there were two trees that would define humankind's journey through time, and they each had strange names: the "Tree of Knowledge of Good and Evil" and "The Tree of Life."

In the creation narrative, God made these two trees along with all the thousands of other trees. And, as God had done after each day of creation, He made the statement that these trees, along with all the others, were good. However, what God has pronounced as good, may not be good for humankind. God said everything that He made was good, even the Tree of Knowledge of Good and Evil. God admired all of the trees He created, as well as the two special trees, and said that all of it was good. But the problem was (and is) that the fruit of the Tree of Knowledge of Good and Evil was (and is) not good *for Adam nor all humankind.* Partaking of its fruit has caused all the problems that exist to this day.

*And out of the ground the Lord God made every tree grow that is pleasant to the sight and good for food. The tree of life was also in the midst of the garden, and the tree of the knowledge of good and evil. Genesis 2:9*

God creates everything. And all throughout the creation narrative, the Bible says that God saw that it was good. On the sixth day, He saw everything that He had made, and indeed it was *very* good! When God was finished with creation, and looked at everything, He said it was not just good but *very* good!

*Then God saw everything that He had made, and indeed it was very good. So the evening and the morning were the sixth day. – Genesis 1:31*

You may have heard of the book of Enoch, who is mentioned in the Bible. He was the 7th generation from Adam. Parts of the book of Enoch were found along with the Dead Sea Scrolls (ancient manuscripts found in the Qumran Caves near the Dead Sea). The book of Enoch is not included in the canon of Scripture, but we do know that it was well-known to people during the time of Jesus and was quoted in Jude 1:14-15 of the New Testament. Enoch gives a bit more description of the Tree of Knowledge of Good and Evil.

According to Enoch, the Tree of Knowledge of Good and Evil was so fragrant that its fragrance spread out through the land. It must have been a grand tree, beautiful to look at and wonderful to smell. Enoch said its fruit resembled grapes. Although we do not build doctrine from the book of Enoch, it does give us additional insight concerning the tree of Knowledge of Good and Evil and states that it was a very beautiful tree.

So, everything that God made was good, even the Tree of Knowledge of Good and Evil was good. The problem was this: *it was not good for Adam or humankind.* Adam was instructed to never eat of that tree. It was very beautiful, very fragrant (according to the Book of Enoch), and very desirable, but the fruit was not meant for humankind and would cause death.

> *And the Lord God commanded the man, saying, "Of every tree of the garden you may freely eat; but of the tree of the knowledge of good and evil you shall not eat, for in the day that you eat of it you shall surely die." – Genesis 2:16-17*

Here we learn that Adam and Eve would die if they ate of the Tree of Knowledge of Good and Evil. They were told not to eat of it. They could freely eat from any tree except that one. There must have been thousands and thousands of trees they could eat from. But there was only one tree that would cause death. There was only one tree that was not good for them.

The question of the ages is, "Why would Adam and Eve eat from the Tree of Knowledge of Good and Evil… why were they tempted?" We are going to look at this a little closer and see if we can gain some insight. But first let's look at the other special tree.

The Genesis narrative provides us with two trees that have names. We have looked at the Tree of Knowledge of Good and Evil, but there is another tree in the narrative that is even more important: The Tree of Life. The Tree of Life would give eternal life to anyone who ate of its fruit. It too was a grand tree. The Book of Enoch give us a description saying that it also had *"a fragrance beyond all fragrance; its leaves and bloom and wood wither not forever; its fruit is beautiful and resembles the dates of a palm." – Book of Enoch 24:4*

Obviously, the Tree of Life was a magnificent tree as well. We really can only imagine. But according to Enoch it too had a wonderful fragrance, and its fruit was like dates. It had the power to give eternal life and must have been magnificent.

Throughout the Bible there are many comparisons to a tree of life. Proverbs says that wisdom is a tree of life…

> *Happy is the man who finds wisdom, And the man who gains understanding; For her proceeds are better than the profits of silver, And her gain than fine gold. She is more precious than rubies, And all the things you may desire cannot compare with her. Length of days is in her right hand, In her left hand riches and honor. Her ways are ways of pleasantness, And all her paths are peace. She is a tree of life to those who take hold of her, And happy are all who retain her. – Proverbs 3:13-18*

Here we learn that wisdom is better than money and jewels. In a world where money seems to be king, the Bible tells us that wisdom is much more valuable than material gain. Even Christians can get caught up in acquiring and accumulating for wealth's sake. We would be wise to pursue wisdom, and only from that vantage point can we truly succeed.

We also learn that wisdom produces long life or "length of days." Many people die early because they made bad decisions and did not think through their actions. They started smoking, or drinking, or any of a number of life shortening actives. Wisdom is long life for those who acquire it.

Nothing you desire can compare with wisdom. In wisdom there is peace and pleasantness. In wisdom there is long life and riches. Everything good stems from acquiring wisdom.

In this Scripture we learn that wisdom is a tree of life. The verse is not necessarily talking about the tree in the garden, but it is saying that wisdom is *like* that tree in the garden. The tree of life is health, long life, and riches. It is everything to complete a wonderful life on this earth. So, what is wisdom and how do we acquire it?

Wisdom is more than just good cognitive thinking. Wisdom is more than just a high IQ. Proverbs chapter eight describes wisdom in great detail and gives us a glimpse of wisdom.

*I have been established from everlasting, From the beginning, before there was ever an earth. - Proverbs 8:23*

Proverbs chapter eight describes wisdom as having a personality. Solomon is often considered the wisest man to ever live. But there was someone even wiser. That is Jesus. Jesus personifies wisdom. I believe that this chapter is a clear portrait of an attribute of Jesus Christ. In this excerpt we learn that wisdom was established from everlasting, that it was present from the beginning, even before the earth was created. That is a beautiful picture of the wisdom of Christ.

*Then I was beside Him as a master craftsman; And I was daily His delight, Rejoicing always before Him, Rejoicing in His inhabited world, And my delight was with the sons of men. - Proverbs 8:30-31*

He was with God from the beginning and was a master craftsman. He helped create the world and everything in it. He loved the created world, and His delight was the with the sons of men. He was alive before creation and is still alive today. Christ is our wisdom. We acquire wisdom when we trust and believe in Him.

*...but to those who are called, both Jews and Greeks, Christ the power of God and the wisdom of God. - 1 Corinthians 1:24*

Christ is the wisdom of God to both Jews and Greeks. He is the power that created all things, and He is the wisdom we acquire when we accept Him. Truly if wisdom is a tree of life, then The Tree of Life is Christ.

*But of Him you are in Christ Jesus, who became for us wisdom from God—and righteousness and sanctification and redemption - 1 Corinthians 1:30*

I submit to you that the Tree of Life in the Garden of Eden is a type of Christ. It represents Christ. If Adam would have eaten from that tree he would have had eternal life. Christ gives those who trust in Him eternal life, just like the Tree of Life in the garden.

*And I give them eternal life, and they shall never perish; neither shall anyone snatch them out of My hand. My Father, who has given them to Me, is greater than all; and no one is able to snatch them out of My Father's hand. - John 10:28-29*

Yes, Jesus is the one who possesses the power to make us live forever. When we believe in Him, we have passed from death to life. When we eat of His fruit, we receive eternal life, and Jesus is well able to prevent anything from taking that life away from us once we have received. No one can snatch those who have received eternal life from His hand or from the Father's hand.

In the Genesis narrative we have two trees in the garden. We have the Tree of Life, which I submit to you is a picture of Christ—or you could say it is a picture of the New Covenant, which is consecrated by the blood of Christ and gives us eternal life when we accept Him. If the Tree of Life is a picture of the New Covenant, then what does the Tree of Knowledge of Good and Evil represent?

The Tree of Knowledge of Good and Evil could be called the tree of death. Even though it gives its partakers an understanding of both good and evil, its fruit produces death. It is the opposite of the Tree of Life. The fruit of the Tree of Life produces just what it says: life. The fruit of the Tree of Knowledge of Good and Evil produces death. They are really the antithesis of each other. One produces life, and the other produces death. They are in complete opposition to each other.

We have already learned that the Tree of Life is a picture of Christ who gives life. It is symbolic of the New Covenant. If the Tree of Life is a picture of the New Covenant, could that mean the Tree of Knowledge of Good and Evil is a picture of the Old Covenant? Am I saying that the New Covenant produces life, and the Old Covenant produces death? Let's look at what Scripture says...

> *But if the ministry of death, written and engraved on stones, was glorious, so that the children of Israel could not look steadily at the face of Moses because of the glory of his countenance, which glory was passing away, how will the ministry of the Spirit not be more glorious? For if the ministry of condemnation had glory, the ministry of righteousness exceeds much more in glory. - 2 Corinthians 3:7-9*

In this passage of Scripture Paul is speaking through the inspiration of the Holy Spirit. He identifies the Ten Commandments as "the ministry of death written and engraved on stones." We know that this is referring to the Ten Commandments. They were written on stone with the "finger of God" while Moses was on Mount Sinai. The Bible tells us that when Moses came down the mountain with those commandments that his face shone with the glory of God. They had to put a veil over his face because of the "glory of his countenance." Moses' face shone brightly with the glory of God! It was so bright that the children of Israel could not look steadily at the face of Moses; it was like looking at the sun. They actually had to put a veil on Moses' face so the people could look at him.

The giving of the law was amazing. God was making known what it takes to be righteous. He was showing us how holy He is and how we need to act and think toward Him and our fellow human beings. However, the passage continues to explain that the glory of the Law was "passing away." The Old Covenant was passing away to make room for something even more glorious: the greater glory of the New Covenant! Paul asks the question, "How will the ministry of the Spirit not be more glorious?" The New Covenant is more glorious. It is the better of the two covenants! It is the greater light. It is more glorious than anything that Moses had in the past. The glory on Moses' face was fading because of the greater light of the gospel of Jesus Christ! The New Covenant is far superior to the old!

Paul draws a great distinction between the Old Covenant and the New Covenant in this passage. One covenant brings death (i.e. the ministry of death), and the other brings life (i.e. the ministry of the Spirit). One covenant brings condemnation, and the other brings righteousness. Both covenants are glorious, but one "exceeds" in glory. Just as both trees in the garden were glorious, one covenant was more glorious than the other.

The two trees in the garden easily represent the two covenants. The Tree of Knowledge of Good and Evil is a picture of the Old Covenant, and the Tree of Life is a picture of the New Covent. The fruit of one is death, and the fruit of the other is life.

> *...who also made us sufficient as ministers of the new covenant, not of the letter but of the*

*Spirit; for the letter kills, but the Spirit gives life.*
*– 2 Corinthians 3:6*

We receive the Holy Spirit when we believe in Christ. We are ministers of the New Covenant. Referring to the Old Covenant, Paul says we are not of the letter but of the Spirit. The letter refers to the Old Covenant while the Spirit refers to the New Covenant. One covenant kills, and the other covenant gives life. The Old Covenant (the ministry of death) kills, while the New Covenant (the ministry of righteousness) gives life! Does that make the Old Covenant evil? What does the Bible say?

*What shall we say then? Is the law sin? God forbid. Nay, I had not known sin, but by the law: for I had not known lust, except the law had said, Thou shalt not covet. – Romans 7:7*

The law exposes our sin. It reveals the fact that we fall way short of God's standards. It was given so that we would understand our need for a redeemer. The law exposes our nakedness. It is the ministry of condemnation. It exposes our inability to live a holy life before a holy God. The law was not designed to make us righteous but rather to expose our sin.

I find it interesting that when Adam and Eve ate of the fruit of the Tree of Knowledge of Good and Evil, they realized that they were naked.

*Then the eyes of both of them were opened, and they knew that they were naked; and they sewed fig leaves together and made themselves coverings. – Genesis 3:7*

When they ate of the Tree of Knowledge of Good and Evil they realized that they were naked. They were lacking. Their glory was gone. They were exposed and separated from God. They tried to cover their nakedness, but as the story continues, the coverings they made were insufficient. God Himself would make them skins to cover their nakedness. A sacrifice was now needed so that their nakedness would not be exposed.

In the same way, the law or Old Covenant exposes our sins (i.e. reveals our nakedness), and we are inadequate through our self-effort to cover those sins. No matter how hard we try to keep the law perfectly we will always fall short and continue to be exposed. We need God to provide our covering. God's provision was a sacrifice, even the sacrifice of His own Son.

You see, the Old Covenant, or Law, was unable to supply life because human beings are unable to keep all of its requirements. We (meaning humankind) fall short of the Law's requirements. That is why God instructed sacrifice along with the Law. In the Old Covenant we needed something to cover sin when we fell short of the Law's requirements. As humans, it is inevitable that we will fall short. There must be shedding of blood for the remission of sins. Animal sacrifice was provided so that even through our short comings and inability to fulfill the law we could be made right before God.

I believe that the Tree of Knowledge of Good and Evil exposed Adam and Eve's nakedness, just as the law exposes our spiritual nakedness. The Tree of Knowledge of Good and Evil is a type of the Law and represents the Old Covenant. The two trees in the Garden represent the two covenants. Both trees were pronounced as being good, and everything God made was pronounced as being very good, including the Tree of Knowledge of Good and Evil. But unfortunately, that tree is not good for humankind, and it kills. Just as the law speaks of judgment and condemns us to death, the Tree of Knowledge of Good and Evil speaks of judgment and condemns humankind to death. I believe that tree represents a clear and accurate picture of the Old

Covenant and the Law. The Tree of Knowledge of Good and Evil is truly "the ministry of death." It exposes humankind's nakedness. We should never attempt to reach God through that tree. We are to reach God through the Tree of Life—through Jesus Christ. We are not to eat of The Tree of Knowledge of Good and Evil (the lessor light), but rather we need to eat of the Tree of Life (the greater light)!

In the garden God made provision for man. Everything that man needed was already provided for on the day mankind was made. Including eternal life. As Believers, we need to recognize that even today, God is our provision, and our eternal life. Every day, we need to eat of the Tree of Life (Jesus Christ) and just accept God's provision for righteousness. Trying to earn righteousness through your own works and self-discipline is like eating of the Tree of Knowledge of Good and Evil. It only produces a curse (sweat, pain, and ultimately death). Stay away from it. Instead, live life in Christ, and experience His salvation, and that will produce good works in your life, naturally and effortlessly. Eat of the Tree of Life and experience a life of victory and provision. Knowing that God desires for us to experience the Tree of Life, and to live under the Greater Light is empowering. The Tree of Life will give you assurance in both good times and bad. Eat of that tree!

# Chapter 6
# The Two Sons of Adam

It seems you can't have children without having a little sibling rivalry. The story of Cain and Abel is the epitome of this. I grew up on a farm with a brother and two sisters. My brother and I were only 10 months apart; we are the same age from March to May. When we were kids, we fought all the time (we also had a lot of fun together as well). One day we were fighting about the chores and who was going to do what. We were fighting because my brother was always finding ways to ditch his chores (at least it seemed that way to me), which meant they would inevitably fall on me. Cleaning out the animals bedding was one of my chores, so I had a pitch fork in my hand. My brother had a hoe or a rake (I can't really remember, but two young brothers armed with chore tools is not a good scenario). We were standing out in the middle of the yard yelling and screaming at each other. It was not unusual for us to go to fisticuffs once in a while, but today, I had a pitchfork. I said to my brother,

"If you take one more step toward me, I swear I am going to stab you with this pitchfork."

Well, guess what he did? He stuck his foot out as if to take a step. I didn't hesitate. Now, in my mind, I saw myself thrusting the pitchfork at his foot, but with the prongs going on either side of it, just shy of doing any damage but enough to scare him. That is not what happened.

I thrust the pitchfork at his foot, just like I had seen in my mind. However, the reality of what happened after that was nothing like I had envisioned. Contrary to the expert aim I had conceived, one of the prongs hit his foot dead center and pierced it clean through. The prong went right through the top of his foot, and out the bottom, and pinned his foot to the ground. I immediately felt remorse, and promptly said, "I am so sorry, I will go ahead and do the chores. No problem. You don't have to."

I felt terrible. I had been so upset that I actually stabbed my brother with a pitchfork. Consequently, because of the remorse that I felt, I realized at that moment I actually loved my brother.

Well, anyway, after a tetanus shot and a couple of stitches, my brother healed up just fine. That is the closest I can come to understanding the rivalry between those two brothers Cain and Abel. Cain murdered his brother Abel and it doesn't appear that Cain had any remorse. Let's examine that story just a bit and see if we can find any parallels to the two covenants here.

After Adam and Eve sinned, they were thrown out of the Garden of Eden. Their first son was named Cain. The name Cain has two common meanings. It is often thought to mean spear, or the shaft of a spear. It can also mean acquired or possession. (Abarim Publications, n.d.) Many people think it is the latter that is the best meaning because of the statement Eve made…

*Now Adam knew Eve his wife, and she conceived and bore Cain, and said, "I have acquired a man from the Lord." - Genesis 4:1*

Eve said that she had acquired a man from the Lord. Because of this proclamation, many scholars agree that Cain's name means possession or acquire. It is fitting as

Cain represents the striving of humankind to acquire things. Human beings often strive to acquire good standing with God through what we do. We also strive to acquire possessions. We strive by the work of our hands to accumulate as much as we can throughout our lifetime. But most of all, Cain represents all those who try to acquire righteousness through their works.

Righteousness through works is a picture of the law. The law demands that we strive to keep all the rules and regulations so that God will be pleased with us and bless us. The problem, however, is that we are unable to keep the law; all of our righteous deeds are like filthy rags. Righteousness is never acquired through good works (although we should always be doing good works). We must acquire our righteousness through faith in Jesus Christ and His finished work on the cross. Cain thought he could acquire redemption from God by giving Him a part of his harvest - that which had been grown out of the ground that was cursed. However, there is only one acceptable sacrifice. Our striving and self-sacrifice will never make us righteous. There must be a blood sacrifice. There must be shedding of blood.

*"And according to the law almost all things are purified with blood, and without shedding of blood there is no remission." – Hebrews 9:22*

Abel was Adam and Eve's second son. He was younger than Cain. Abel's name can mean many things. It can mean vapor or breath. It can also mean to act emptily or become vain. (Abarim Publications, n.d.) The context is a short breath. Something that does not last long. Most Hebrew scholars agree that Abel probably means small breath or vapor. He was probably so named because of his short time on this earth. He was the first person to die and the first person to be murdered.

The meaning small breath is interesting. The Bible says that God breathed into Adam and he became a living soul…

*"And the Lord God formed man of the dust of the ground, and breathed into his nostrils the breath of life; and man became a living being."*
*– Genesis 2:7*

The name small breath could be a reference to how God put the final touch on His greatest creation: Adam. We are made in God's image, and we have His breath, which makes us unique. God is the great breath, and we are His small breath. Abel was pleasing to God and certainly an amazing example of the character we should pursue as living beings with the breath of God that was placed within us. Maybe the meaning of Abel is a picture of who we are and our "God-breathed" relationship to God.

The story of Cain and Able can be paralleled to that of the Old Covenant and New Covenant. This account of the first murder is similar to another narrative in a later chapter of Genesis. In chapter sixteen of Genesis a narrative begins concerning the story of two other brothers who did not get along: Ishmael and Isaac. Both narratives relate the animosity of two brothers at odds with each other. One brother is jealous because the other is favored. The book of Galatians gives us insight into these two other brothers…

*"Now we, brethren, as Isaac was, are children of promise. But, as he who was born according to the flesh then persecuted him who was born according to the Spirit, even so it is now." -*
*Galatians 4:28-29*

Speaking of Isaac and Ishmael, the writer of Galatians (Paul) reveals that these two brothers represent the conflict between that which is rejected and that which is accepted. It is the conflict between the Law and the Spirit. It is the conflict between Old Covenant and New Covenant.

I submit to you that the first two brothers (Cain and Abel) mirror this conflict as well. They too are representative of two covenants: one of the Law that condemns and one of the Spirit that gives life. One is rejected; the other is accepted. Thus, through Cain and Abel, begins the struggle for approval. It is an analogy to the question of whether we can receive approval through our works or through the blood of an innocent sacrifice.

When Christ came, the Pharisees and Sadducees, who were huge proponents of the Old Covenant, were not happy with any potential change to their way of life. They ended up rejecting Jesus and having Him crucified. Jesus was put to death by His fellow Jews, or "brothers." When Cain killed his brother Abel it was a shadow, or picture, of Jesus being rejected and put to death by His brothers (the Jews).

Another interesting parallel to Christ is that after Jesus had died, to make sure He was dead, one of the soldiers at the cross pierced Him with a spear. The name Cain can mean spear, and certainly Cain made sure that Abel was dead.

Also, just like Abel's name is often thought to represent a short life, Jesus was not on this earth long. Jesus died somewhere close to 33 years of age. He was a sacrifice for our sin, and just as God accepted the sacrifice which Abel presented, God has accepted the sacrifice of His Son.

Now, here is something to ponder. For Cain to be accepted, he could have brought a blood sacrifice like Abel did. But he didn't. God accepted Abel's sacrifice but not Cain's offering. Cain brought the work of his hands, while Abel brought blood. However, eventually, Cain did bring blood, but it was his brother's blood through murder that was spilled.

Although Abel is a picture of Christ, his blood is not like the blood of Jesus. Abel's blood is tainted with sin. It is tainted with the sin he inherited from his father Adam. So, the blood of Abel cries out for vengeance. It cries out for retribution.

*...to Jesus the Mediator of the new covenant, and to the blood of sprinkling that speaks better things than that of Abel. – Hebrews 12:24*

Yet, how is it that the Scripture says that Abel was righteous if he was born of sin? God declared Abel as righteous because of his faith. Righteousness always comes by faith, even in the Old Covenant.

> *By faith Abel offered to God a more excellent sacrifice than Cain, through which he obtained witness that he was righteous, God testifying of his gifts; and through it he being dead still speaks. Hebrews 11:4*

The law is righteous, and holy, and just. The problem is that the law cannot make us righteous, or holy, or just. Abel was a righteous man, but his blood cries out for vengeance. That is what the law does. It condemns us because we are unable to live up to its standards. The law cannot bring redemption. The Old Testament law was unable to produce righteousness in humankind. But where the law is weak, Christ is strong.

Cain killed Abel, and Abel's blood cries out for vengeance. But the blood of Christ speaks better things! The blood of Jesus speaks MERCY! Just as Abel was rejected by his brother, Christ was rejected by the spiritual leaders of His own nation (His brothers so to speak).

The writer of the book of Hebrews points out a parallel between the blood of Abel and the blood of

Christ. I see a similarity between the gospel narrative and the story of Cain and Abel. You can draw a correlation between Cain and the Old Covenant (the Law). You can also draw a correlation between Abel and Christ or the New Covenant. The older (Law or Old Covenant) persecutes the younger (Grace or New Covenant). Both Christ and Abel are persecuted because of their favor with God and are eventually killed by their persecutors.

Let's look at some of the narrative in Genesis...

*...Now Abel was a keeper of sheep, but Cain was a tiller of the ground. Genesis 4:2*

It is very easy to read right through this verse. But let's take a close look at it. Abel was a keeper of sheep. That means that Abel was a shepherd. Throughout all of Scripture a shepherd is often a picture of Christ.

*"The LORD is my shepherd; I shall not want."*
*- Psalms 23:1*

King David was a shepherd and least in his household. Yet, he was the anointed king of Israel. David would risk his life for his flock all the time. He fought off lions and bears to keep his sheep safe. David too, is a type of Christ.

*For thus says the Lord GOD: "Indeed I Myself will search for My sheep and seek them out. As a shepherd seeks out his flock on the day he is among his scattered sheep, so will I seek out My sheep and deliver them from all the places where they were scattered on a cloudy and dark day." - Ezekiel 34:11-12*

God often likens Himself as a shepherd. It is a picture of His love and devotion to His people. Jesus referred to himself as the good shepherd.

*I am the good shepherd. The good shepherd gives His life for the sheep. - John 10:11*

In contrast, Cain was a tiller of the ground. He was a farmer. He worked the ground to produce fruit. The law is much like that. To live by the law, we must continually discipline ourselves to follow each and every demand. Because we are made of dust, in a sense, when we apply the law for righteousness, we are tilling the ground. We are removing weeds and making sure that we don't allow something to sprout up which could "stunt our growth" so to speak. The law is the tool that we use to till our bodies which are made of the earth.

*If you walk in My statutes and keep My commandments, and perform them, then I will give you rain in its season, the land shall yield its produce, and the trees of the field shall yield their fruit. Your threshing shall last till the time of vintage, and the vintage shall last till the time of sowing; you shall eat your bread to the full, and dwell in your land safely. - Leviticus 26:3-5*

In this Scripture, keeping the law produces a great physical harvest. The problem is that humankind is unable to keep the law; thus, the law is unable to make one righteous. The law can only produce condemnation and death. On the other hand, in Christ we experience all blessing. In Christ, our ground is made fruitful, and we produce a great harvest! In Christ, the curse of the ground is removed, and we experience the fruit of righteousness.

So, in each of the brother's vocation, we can see a picture of Old and New Covenant. One represents Christ and the other the law. Now it is easy to see why God accepts one but not the other.

*And in the process of time it came to pass that Cain brought an offering of the fruit of the ground to the Lord. Abel also brought of the firstborn of his flock and of their fat. And the Lord respected Abel and his offering, but He did not respect Cain and his offering. And Cain was very angry, and his countenance fell. – Genesis 4:3-5*

So, Abel offers the blood of an innocent lamb. It is the only acceptable offering. Cain offers the works of his hands. The fruit of his labor that is never acceptable as a covering for sin. There must be blood shed for the remission of sin. Abel understood this, but Cain obviously did not.

As a consequence, Cain's countenance fell. He was very upset. He did not understand atonement. He thought that his offering should be every bit as acceptable as his brothers. This is often the response from those who think that righteousness is by works. They believe that their hard work should be counted as equal to that of innocent blood. But it is not. Innocent blood is the only thing that can make us acceptable to God. Blood is the only atonement for sin. Abel understood this.

*"Do not be deceived, God is not mocked; for whatever a man sows, that he will also reap. For he who sows to his flesh will of the flesh reap corruption, but he who sows to the Spirit will of the Spirit reap everlasting life. And let us not grow weary while doing good, for in due season we shall reap if we do not lose heart." - Galatians 6:7-9*

Cain sowed to his flesh, which is really made of dust or the ground. He is a picture of humankind attempting to be righteous through works. Fleshly discipline never produces righteousness. We must sow to the Spirt. We must accept the atonement of blood that Jesus provided. Only then will we be made righteous. Trusting in the blood of Jesus will produce a great spiritual harvest of righteousness! Then we will be accepted and counted in the "Hall of Faith" (Hebrews Chapter 11), just as Abel was! His sacrifice was the greater light.

*"In this the children of God and the children of the devil are manifest: Whoever does not practice righteousness is not of God, nor is he who does not love his brother. For this is the message that you heard from the beginning, that we should love one another, not as Cain who was of the wicked one and murdered his brother. And why did he murder him? Because his works were evil and his brother's righteous. - I John 3:10-12 NKJV*

# Chapter 7
# The Two Wives of Abraham

The two wives of Abraham are certainly a clear analogy of the two covenants. Paul clearly identifies these two women as being symbolic of the two covenants. We will go over that analogy, but first I want to clarify something that I believe is important to understand. Just because a portion of Scripture is identified as being an analogy, or a symbolic picture of a spiritual truth, does not diminish the validity of the historical narrative of the text. Abraham and his wives, Sarah and Hagar were real people who lived out their lives shortly after the flood of Noah. Interestingly, Abraham could easily have known and talked with Noah. Abraham was about fifty-eight years old when Noah died at the age of nine hundred fifty. That is the beauty of Scripture. Not only do we read literal historical fact (like in the life of Abraham), but God uses these stories to present the gospel to anyone who has "eyes to see."

The Bible often uses historical narrative to present spiritual truth. The Bible is a masterpiece of multiple writers from different backgrounds whose writings span across many centuries and who have all written about the one true God. They have written consistently and accurately, with many of the historical narratives paralleling the gospel of Christ.

Scripture is the living word of God and is meant to educate and challenge us, but most of all it is designed to bring us into a better relationship with Him and to learn His thoughts toward us. Consider the following Scripture…

*You shall not muzzle an ox while it treads out the grain. – Deuteronomy 25:4*

In this passage, God was clarifying the law and providing the Jewish people with practical application so they could have a clear understanding to live by. Here God tells the Jewish people that if an ox is treading out grain, they should make sure to allow the ox to eat from the grain that falls along his path. You are not to keep the ox from eating by putting a muzzle on him. Most Jewish people would find doing such a thing counterproductive as the ox needs to keep his strength so that more grain is treaded out. But if someone borrowed an ox from its owner and wanted to make sure he maximized his profit, he may be inclined to return the oxen hungry. So, God makes sure that the propensity to maximize profit at the expense of an animal is addressed and preserves it in Scripture.

It is true that the Jewish people used oxen to tread out grain. This is a historical fact. But, this fact can also teach us something about God's heart and how He wants us to live. Look what Paul says…

*For it is written in the law of Moses, "You shall not muzzle an ox while it treads out the grain." Is it oxen God is concerned about? Or does He say it altogether for our sakes? For our sakes, no doubt, this is written, that he who plows should plow in hope, and he who threshes in hope should be partaker of his hope. If we have sown spiritual things for you, is it a great thing*

So, you see? The law in Deuteronomy is teaching us a greater truth; something much greater than taking care of animals. That is, our spiritual leaders, who are treading out the nourishment of the Word, are entitled to provision from those to whom they share that Word with. Actually, we learn that God was not only concerned about the oxen, but He preserved this law to teach us something! It is written, not only for oxen, but more importantly for us. We have this Scripture, written to us, in order that we take care of those who provide our nourishment, both physical and spiritual. Here, you can see how the Word of God is living! It had meaning for those when it was written and also fresh meaning for us who read it 3,000 years later!

The narrative of the two wives of Abraham is not only written to record history but is also an amazing analogy of the two covenants. It is historically accurate and is quite an outstanding picture of law and grace-- of the Old Covenant and the New Covenant. So, let's look at the narrative a bit.

Most of you know the story. God promises Abraham that he would be the father of many nations. Abraham was 75 years old when God made this known to him. Time passed, and when Abraham was 86 Sarah grew tired of waiting and asked Abraham to sleep with her hand maiden, Hagar, so that she might have a son through her servant. Of course, Abraham obliged and did sleep with Hagar. He had a son and named him Ishmael. This, however, was not God's plan. God would eventually give Abraham a son through Sarah. That was God's plan all along. So, when Abraham was 100 years old, he indeed had a son through Sarah. They named him Isaac.

Isaac was the son that God had promised Abraham. God made sure that Abraham and Sarah were well past childbearing age before Sarah conceived. Isaac was truly a miracle son from God as the Bible says that Sarah and Abraham were dead (so to speak).

*And not being weak in faith, he did not consider his own body, already dead (since he was about a hundred years old), and the deadness of Sarah's womb. He did not waver at the promise of God through unbelief, but was strengthened in faith, giving glory to God, and being fully convinced that what He had promised He was also able to perform. – Romans 4:19*

According to this Scripture Abraham and Sarah were both unable to produce offspring. Isaac was the son of promise brought through a miracle of God. God had made it so that Abraham and Sarah were able to conceive. God's restoration of their ability to conceive is a type of resurrection, so to speak.

Ishmael (son of the bondwoman), who was born 16 years before Isaac (son of the free woman), was a direct result of human effort through Abraham's relations with Hagar; Sarah's servant. Ishmael represents the product of Abraham's own works and abilities. On the other hand, Isaac represents the power of the Spirit of God to produce life from death. So, Ishmael represents the works of the flesh while Isaac represents the works of God.

These two sons represent the two covenants. Ishmael represents the Old Covenant of law. Law demands righteousness from humankind. People are expected to keep the law, so that they can maintain a relationship with God. The law is completely flesh-based. It requires sheer will power and effort from human beings to keep its requirements. And if they don't, it could mean death.

Isaac represents the New Covenant, or the Covenant of Grace. Grace supplies righteousness to humankind through the finished work of Christ. People simply need to believe in Jesus Christ and His righteousness is imputed to the person who believes. Just as Isaac was a product of God working in the life of Abraham and Sarah, so our righteousness is a product of Christ's work on the cross. We are of the Spirit just as Isaac is of the Spirit.

This is not a loose analogy. The Book of Galatians and Romans confirm that the life of Abraham and the story of his wives are a picture of the two covenants. Paul provides us with insight into Abraham's life through the book of Galatians…

> *For it is written that Abraham had two sons: the one by a bondwoman, the other by a freewoman. – Galatians 4:22*

Notice that Paul, inspired by the Holy Spirit, says one wife was a bondwoman and the other a freewoman. Hagar was the bondwoman. She was not the one Abraham loved. She was the servant of Sarah. The bondwoman must submit to the freewoman and do what she says. The bondwoman was a slave and her offspring would not have the same inheritance as the child of the proper and legal wife (Sarah).

> *But he who was of the bondwoman was born according to the flesh, and he of the freewoman through promise, which things are symbolic. - Galatians 4:23-24*

This New Testament Scripture tells us how the story of the two wives of Abraham are symbolic. One of the children was born of the bondwoman according to the flesh. That is referring to Abraham having sex with Hagar and trying to produce a son for Sarah from his own effort. Little did Abraham know that his decision would produce much heartache and pain for the Jewish people even to this day.

The other son was of the freewoman and was the result of a miracle. It was a fulfillment of the promise God had made to Abraham years before Isaac was born. Sarah was Abraham's proper and legal wife. She was not a servant like Hagar. The son born through her was a miracle and indeed a manifestation of the Spirit working in Abraham and Sarah's life.

Notice also that Paul explains that these things are symbolic. The nation of Israel was born through Abraham's son Isaac, but in bringing that promise to pass, God weaved the gospel message through the lives of Abraham's wives. Now, Paul explains the symbolism...

> *For these are the two covenants: the one from Mount Sinai which gives birth to bondage, which is Hagar— for this Hagar is Mount Sinai in Arabia, and corresponds to Jerusalem which now is, and is in bondage with her children— but the Jerusalem above is free, which is the mother of us all. – Galatians 4:24-26*

One wife represents the earthly Jerusalem, or Mount Sinai, where Moses received the law, and the other represents the New Jerusalem, or Mount Zion!

> *But you have come to Mount Zion and to the city of the living God, the heavenly Jerusalem, to an innumerable company of angels, - Hebrews 12:22*

Clearly, we see that Hagar is a picture of the Old Covenant of law. We learn from these Scriptures that the bondwoman is symbolic of the law and the free woman is symbolic of the work of Christ on the cross!

The bondwoman is a servant of the freewoman, and therefore we conclude that the Old Covenant is the servant of the New Covenant. Not the other way around. Somehow early in my Christian life, I had pictured the gift of the Holy Spirit as being given to Christians so that we would have power to keep the law. I thought God gave the Spirit so we could follow the law. That was a grave error.

The Holy Spirit is given as a seal of our righteousness through Christ. It is a like a down payment ensuring that God will fulfill His promise of eternal life.

> *"In Him you also trusted, after you heard the word of truth, the gospel of your salvation; in whom also, having believed, you were sealed with the Holy Spirit of promise, who is the guarantee of our inheritance until the redemption of the purchased possession, to the praise of His glory." – Ephesians 1:13-14*

The Spirit within every believer is a pledge given as a gift for trusting in the finished work of the cross. The grace and power of God is immensely greater than the self-discipline of humankind. Our trust must always be in the power of His Spirit, and not our own abilities.

So, we see that the two wives of Abraham are a picture of the Old and New Testament. Again, we have an amazing analogy of the gospel in the life of Abraham. Sarah is a representation of the assurance of God's promises and His faithfulness to carry them out in His good timing. As Christians our mother (so to speak) is Sarah, the free woman! We are not of Hagar, the bond woman. One wife is certainly the better of the two or the greater light (so to speak)!

> *"So then, brethren, we are not children of the bondwoman but of the free. – Galatians 4:31*

# Chapter 8
# The Two Kinds of Wine Skins

Many people have an aversion to change. Some people are very resistant to adopting a new idea or any different approach to a familiar task even if it means that it would be more efficient and less taxing on them. For example, my wife does not consider Google when she has a question about something. She would much rather go to the library or call a friend who may have more knowledge on the issue. She still writes out her grocery list with pen and paper while younger wives use an iPhone app or order their groceries online to pick them up later. She says,

"The old way is better. I prefer a pen and paper. I like to write."

She currently uses an iPhone, but it took me years of nagging her and pushing her to switch from her old flip phone to an iPhone. Once she switched and spent some time learning it, she loved it. But she does not like to adopt new things. She has an aversion to any new process or technology or way of thinking.

The Pharisees and Sadducees had the same aversion to Jesus' teachings.

*Then they said to Him, "Why do the disciples of John fast often and make prayers, and likewise those of the Pharisees, but Yours eat and drink?" – Luke 5:33*

The spiritual leaders of the time could not understand Jesus' perspective. He was teaching them the "spirit" of the law and not the "letter" of the law. He was teaching them how people should consider each other. He was not concerned as much with outward appearances, but rather He was focused on matters of the heart.

Over the years the Jewish people had experienced both great hardship and great blessing. When they served God, they would experience incredible blessing and prosperity. But if they strayed after other gods, they experienced great heartache and were often given over to their enemies. And each time they were given over to their enemies, they would eventually repent, and God would bless them again. The Pharisees and Sadducees came about as a result of the vacillating loyalty to God. The spiritual leaders of Jesus' day were there to prevent Israel from straying away from God so that they would not experience the defeat of their enemies (Neusner, 1973).

Most of those leaders were very dedicated to the law of Moses. They considered Moses to be the greatest man who ever lived. They had studied the law and developed tradition that would help them keep God's law to the letter. But in doing so, they forgot the intent of the law. They forgot why the law existed. Their trust was actually in their own ability and self-discipline to keep the law perfectly. They revered Moses and held him in very high esteem. But there was someone better than Moses, and they had an aversion to Him and His teachings.

*For the law was given through Moses, but grace and truth came through Jesus Christ. – John 1:17*

Here we learn that God gave the Jewish people the Law through Moses. Grace and truth came through Jesus Christ. Grace and truth are not like the stone that the Law was written on. Grace and truth CAME. Grace and truth are in the person of Jesus Christ. He is grace and truth! The law was given by a servant, but grace and truth came through the Son. The law was given through a mediator, but Jesus Christ is our High Priest full of grace and truth. One covenant came by a servant and the other covenant came by the Son of God. Which is greater?

To the people of Israel, Moses was the greatest person who ever lived. When Christians put Jesus higher than Moses, it was something that many of the Israelites took issues with. They could not give up Moses for Christ. To the Jews, no one was greater than Moses. In their minds there was no greater leader than Moses whom they had studied and heard about for centuries. But through Christ all things become new.

> *For this One has been counted worthy of more glory than Moses, inasmuch as He who built the house has more honor than the house. For every house is built by someone, but He who built all things is God. And Moses indeed was faithful in all His house as a servant, for a testimony of those things which would be spoken afterward, but Christ as a Son over His own house, whose house we are if we hold fast the confidence and the rejoicing of the hope firm to the end. - Hebrews 3:3-6*

Jesus is worthy of more glory. Moses was a servant of the house, but the builder of the house had come! The builder has more glory than the servant. The builder is the Son, and He is the owner of the house. It was time to let go of the old and make room for the new.

This was not going to be easy for the Jewish leaders. Jesus lived His life in front of them doing good works and miracles which give credibility to His authority. His works were a testimony that He was the Son of God. All of His miracles and teaching were done to reveal that He was the creator. It was He who was on Mount Sinai with Moses, and it was He who wrote the law. So, consequently, He was well qualified to interpret the law and to bring about a New Covenant. One that was not based on the blood of bulls and goats--but a new covenant based on Jesus' own blood.

As the Pharisees questioned his teaching and methods, Jesus presented two parables to illuminate what was taking place at that time and what He was bringing to the Jewish Nation. The first parable is about a garment.

*Then He spoke a parable to them: "No one puts a piece from a new garment on an old one; otherwise the new makes a tear, and also the piece that was taken out of the new does not match the old. – Luke 5:36*

Today we don't patch clothing like they used to. We just go get another pair of jeans or a new shirt. Everything is disposable in this day and age. But I can remember when I was a kid, we patched all of our cloths. We seldom went and purchased new clothing. I remember my Mom patching my jeans. She would always use material that had been washed already. If she used new material to patch a hole, the patch would shrink in the wash. It would pull the old material tight and could easily tear an even bigger hole when I wore it. Mom always used patch material that had been washed several times.

Jesus was talking about the New Covenant that He was bringing. Moses had brought the Old Covenant and the Law, but Jesus was bringing something new. The old cloth is a picture of the Old Covenant. Trying to patch the Old Covenant with the New Covenant will not work. It will only tear it to pieces. The new piece does not match the old. There will be no patching up something that already existed. It was time for a new garment!

Jesus was saying that they must be made new. He was not just bringing a patch. He was bringing something greater than the old cloth. It was not good to apply what He was teaching to their existing understanding, but rather they needed to see His teaching through a new way of looking at the law. The things that Jesus was teaching tears to pieces the "letter" of the law. His teaching was much deeper, reaching into the "spirit" of the law. If they tried to understand Christ's teaching through any perspective other than through the "spirit" of the law it only created friction and tearing. It was time for them to move from the "letter" of the Law to the "spirit" of the Law. That is what it would take to really grasp what Jesus is saying.

> *...who also made us sufficient as ministers of the new covenant, not of the letter but of the Spirit; for the letter kills, but the Spirit gives life.*
> *– 2 Corinthians 3:6*

There is a difference between the Old Covenant and the New Covenant, just as there is a difference between the old cloth and the new cloth. We must embrace the New Covenant. We are ministers of the New Covenant, and often it's teachings can cause a tear or a rift in those who still cling to the Old Covenant Law. The message of "righteousness through faith" can cause tension with those who believe they must be self-disciplined with good works in order to be right before God.

Jesus gave us another parable similar to the two types of cloth. This parable is much more familiar to most Christians than the two types of cloth. It is the two types of wine skins.

> *And no one puts new wine into old wineskins; or else the new wine will burst the wineskins and be spilled, and the wineskins will be ruined.*

*But new wine must be put into new wineskins, and both are preserved. And no one, having drunk old wine, immediately desires new; for he says, 'The old is better.' – Luke 5:37-39*

Jesus told the parable of the wineskins right after the parable of the two cloths. It has a similar meaning. It is a representation of the two covenants. There are two types of wine skins: old and new. I believe that the wineskins represent people under two different covenants.

*Also for Adam and his wife the Lord God made tunics of skin, and clothed them. – Genesis 3:21*

When Adam and Eve tried to cover themselves with fig leaves, it was not sufficient. God had to make them skins of animals. He clothed them in skins. Humankind's effort to cover themselves is never enough. They must have the covering that God provides, and that covering requires the shedding of blood. God had to kill animals to make skins for Adam and Eve. Blood had to be shed so that their sin would not be held against them. They were then covered with those skins of the animals that had shed their blood.

Just as the parable mentions wineskins that have wine poured into them, Jesus was pouring out of Himself to all the people. He is the new wine that is being poured out. Those who were steeped in the Old Covenant were unable to accept His teaching, but those who were sinners and even Gentiles accepted His healing and teaching gladly. The Old Covenant "wine skins" were cracking and breaking under the teaching (or new wine) of Jesus.

In the New Testament there were two people whom Jesus said had great faith. Their faith was even greater than He had seen in Israel. Both of those people were Gentiles. The two people who had the greatest faith in the New Testament during Jesus' time here on earth were not people of the Old Covenant but rather "new wineskins" for whom he poured out His healing.

*"And thou shalt make a covering for the tent of rams' skins dyed red, and a covering above of badgers' skins," - Ex 26:14*

Skins were also used for the tabernacle. Each skin represented something. The rams' skins dyed red are a symbol of Christ Blood that was shed for us. Those ram skins dyed red encased the Holy of Holies where the Spirit of God was. Now, His Spirit is within us. I believe that the wineskins in Jesus' parable represent people. Some are old wineskins still under law, and those who accept Christ are made new (new wineskins) and filled with the new wine of His Spirit.

Wine is often considered a symbol of joy in Scripture.

*You have put gladness in my heart, more than in the season that their grain and wine increased. – Psalm 4:7*

In the Bible, new wine is a picture of joy and gladness. It was a blessing to enjoy new wine and a curse when there was no new wine. Jesus' first miracle was to turn the water into wine at the wedding feast. That was the first picture of what Jesus was about to do in His ministry. The pots that used to hold the water for cleansing would be converted to wine containers! What used to be an arduous task of cleansing would be converted to a source of joy. No longer would we need the cleansing through ceremony but rather we would now be made clean when we partake of the New Wine of the Spirit of God through Jesus Christ.

Jesus was bringing a new and better way. The Pharisees and Sadducees were unable to accept it. They represent the old wineskins that burst. They represent the

Old Covenant ways, and anything new was completely rejected and only caused irritation and threatened the long traditions that had evolved from the Old Covenant.

The New Wine skins are those people who are not stretched and aged by the Old Covenant. They are those who are pliable. They are those who can accept the New Covenant that was brought through Jesus Christ.

> *Therefore, if anyone is in Christ, he is a new creation; old things have passed away; behold, all things have become new. – 2 Corinthians 5:17*

To be in Christ is to have the old replaced by the new. We become new when we receive the Holy Spirit. We are not of the Old Covenant. We are not "old wineskins." We are of the New Covenant, and we are "new wineskins," full of joy and the Holy Spirit!

Many scholars hold to this interpretation of this parable. They believe that the Old wineskins and the old cloth represent the Old Covenant and the law while the new cloth and new wineskins represent the New Covenant and grace. (Bruce, 1983) (Lachs, 1987) (Lenski, 1961) (Stern, 1992). There is such a general consensus to this interpretation that you will often hear people use the term "old wine" as a figure of speech to refer to the Old Covenant.

So, here is an analogy of the Old Covenant and New Covenant in these two parables. We learn here that Christ was bringing something new and better, and how important it was to be open to His ministry, and the conformation of it through miracles and the resurrection. Again, we see through these parables that the New Covenant is truly the greater light!

# Chapter 9
# The Two Kinds of Christians

There are many pictures and analogies of the two covenants in the Bible. It is a unique book in that it presents the gospel repeatedly through songs, stories, historical narrative, and even genealogies. From Genesis to Revelation, we see many, many pictures of the two covenants: the covenant of law and the covenant of grace - and one is always greater than the other!

From the first chapter in Genesis, we see how God introduced us to the two great lights. He made clear that one light was greater than the other. One light was to rule the day, and the other light was to rule the night. From creation to the new heaven and the new earth, the scripture clearly reveals to us that Christ is the greater light. He is the one who rules the day. The law does not rule; it only reveals our sin. It is Christ who rules, and it was His joy to be the work of redemption for us. It was His joy to provide rest from our constant striving for righteousness.

In my opinion, there are really two types of Christians: one who lives by law, and another who lives by grace. The Christian who lives by the law is always striving to please God. That person believes God is only pleased with them when they do right or when they have not made any mistakes. And, if they do make a mistake, they must ask forgiveness, or they are in danger of going to hell. They live in a perpetual cycle of sometimes being good and sometimes not so good. They are up and down. Never quite sure if they measure up to God's high standard. That is not how God intended us to live.

The other type of Christian is the one who recognizes that they are unable to live up to the high standard of the law. They realize that they are only made righteous through the precious blood of Jesus Christ. They recognize that they are right with God, not because of what they have done, but rather because of what Jesus has done. They recognize that Jesus blood is greater than the law and the blood of animal sacrifices. The sinless blood of Christ is what makes them acceptable to God. They live in the sure victory of the cross, recognizing that they (themselves) fall short, but their Lord and King (Jesus) has defeated the giant that has taunted them. Just as David defeated Goliath, and all Israel reaped the benefit, Jesus has defeated sin and death, and all Christians benefit!

> *"There is therefore now no condemnation to those who are in Christ Jesus, who do not walk according to the flesh, but according to the Spirit. For the law of the Spirit of life in Christ Jesus has made me free from the law of sin and death. For what the law could not do in that it was weak through the flesh, God did by sending His own Son in the likeness of sinful flesh, on account of sin: He condemned sin in the flesh, that the righteous requirement of the law might be fulfilled in us who do not walk according to the flesh but according to the Spirit." – Romans 8:1-4*

It is Christ who is the greater light, and we need to walk confidently in that light, knowing that the work of Christ is greater than the work of man. Just as the sun is greater than the moon, the New Covenant is greater than the Old Covenant. It is through the New Covenant that we are acceptable to God and can live a victorious life. The righteousness of Christ has been imputed upon us and has made us part of the family of God and joint heirs with Christ!

The gospel is the great message of hope: that human beings can be righteous before God, and approach His throne with boldness, knowing that their redeemer has conquered sin and death. Jesus has done all the work. He has paid all the price. There is no more work to do. There is no more price to pay. We have entered the kingdom of heaven and nothing can take that away from us.

> *"And I give them eternal life, and they shall never perish; neither shall anyone snatch them out of My hand. My Father, who has given them to Me, is greater than all; and no one is able to snatch them out of My Father's hand. I and My Father are one." – John 10:28-30*

God gave the nation of Israel the covenant of the law on Mount Sinai. He gave the covenant of grace on Mount Zion. One covenant is written on stone, and the other is written on our hearts. One mountain is full of smoke and fire, and anyone who touches it will die. The other is full of grace and truth, and those who touch it will live! You see... it is no longer our strength and discipline that make us righteous, but rather the strength and discipline that Jesus walked in! When you realize this simple truth, you enter His rest. You enter a relationship that takes the pressure off you and replaces it with assurance of salvation and the anticipation of blessing and favor!

There is a new spring in the step of the Christian that grabs hold of this revelation. There is a new joy in the believer that recognizes the absolute finished work of the cross. The Bible begins to come alive again with pictures of Christ and His victory. You begin to see it in every chapter and verse. It is like coming out of the dark and into the light. It is like eating of the tree of life! It is the new wine in new wine skins! Your Christian walk takes on a new meaning. Your relationship with Him becomes fresh and alive! Just like when you were first saved, and it never goes away. You begin to live in the victory that God always intended for your life. The gospel is truly "good news!"

I wrote this book because I remember the joy I felt when I came to realize that all my striving for God's favor was not necessary. He loved me already. He loved me while I was a sinner and sent Christ to die for me (and you). It is all Him and none of me. It is all Him, and none of you!

I pray that this book has helped you to see that you are loved by God and that you have entered His rest, and there is no need to strive for His approval. You already have it. I pray that your good works stem from the joy that is within you and not from a need to find approval. I pray that this book helps to make the Bible come alive with pictures of the gospel all throughout the Old and New Testament. I pray that you begin to see there is a greater light and a lesser light and that the greater light is the better of the two. I pray that you live in that greater light, and that light will shine brightly everywhere that God leads you.

# *Works Cited*

*10 Great Jewish Contributions to Mankind.* (n.d.). Retrieved from historyandheadlines.com: http://www.historyandheadlines.com/10-great-jewish-contributions-mankind/

Abarim Publications. (n.d.). *Abel Meaning*. Retrieved October 7, 2016, from http://www.abarim-publications.com/Meaning/Abel.html

Abarim Publications. (n.d.). *Cain Meaning*. Retrieved October 7, 2016, from http://www.abarim-publications.com/Meaning/Cain.html

Bruce, F. F. (1983). *Hard Sayings of Yeshua.* Downers Grove, Il: IV Press. Retrieved 11 08, 2016

Cronin, B. (n.d.). *The 10 Most Expensive Comic Books Ever Sold.* Retrieved December 12, 2019, from CBR.com: http://www.cbr.com/the-10-most-expensive-comic-books-ever-sold/

Dictionary.com. (1995). *Dictionary.com.* Retrieved August 1, 2016

EarthSky. (2013, June 26). *Coincidence that sun and moon seem same size?* Retrieved August 1, 2016, from earthsky.org: http://earthsky.org/space/coincidence-that-sun-and-moon-seem-same-size

Evans, E. (n.d.). *Tree Facts.* Retrieved September 20, 2016, from NCSU.edu: https://www.ncsu.edu/project/treesofstrength/trefact.htm

Goriss, L. (2016, September 02). *Jewish Contributions to Society.* Retrieved September 20, 2016, from judaism.about.com: http://judaism.about.com/od/culture/a/contribution.htm

Hays, J. (2015, June). *Christians In Singapore*. Retrieved September 20, 2016, from FactsAndDetails.com: http://factsanddetails.com/southeast-asia/Singapore/sub5_7a/entry-3721.html

Homans, D. J. (2015, March 20). *35,000 Decisions: The Great Choices of Strategic Leaders*. Retrieved September 23, 2016, from Roberts Wesleyan College: http://go.roberts.edu/leadingedge/the-great-choices-of-strategic-leaders

ICv2. (2011). *Amazing Fantasy #15 Sells For $1.1 Million*. Retrieved December 12, 2019, from https://icv2.com/articles/comics/view/19588/am azing-fantasy-15-sells-1-1-million

Julia Layton & Craig Freudenrich, P. (2000, 10 17). *How the Sun Works*. Retrieved 07 18, 2018, from https://science.howstuffworks.com/sun.htm

Lachs, S. T. (1987). *A Rabbinic Commentary on the New Testament*. Hoboken, NJ: Ktav Publishing House, Inc. Retrieved 11 08, 2016

Lenski, R. (1961). *The Interpretation of Luke's Gospel*. Minneapolis, MN: Augsburg Publishing House. Retrieved 11 08, 2016

Neusner, J. (1973). *From Politics to Piety: The Emergence of Pharisaic Judaism*. Englewood Cliffs, NJ: Prentice-Hall, Inc.

Pease, S. L. (2009). *The Golden Age of Jewish Achievement*. Deucalion.

Reference.com. (n.d.). *How Many Moons Would Fit Inside The Sun?* Retrieved September 20, 2016, from Reference.com: https://www.reference.com/science/many-moons-would-fit-inside-sun-f2975e863f753252#

Spencer, D. A. (2017, July 14). *How Christian Missionaries Changed the World for the Better*. Retrieved July 17, 2018, from https://tifwe.org/how-christian-missionaries-changed-the-world-for-the-better/

Stern, R. H. (1992). *The New American Commentary, Volume 24 Luke*. Nashville, TN: Broadman Press. Retrieved 11 08, 2016

Thornhill, W. (2010, 03 1). *Our Misunderstood Sun*. Retrieved 07 18, 2018, from http://www.holoscience.com/wp/our-misunderstood-sun/

Woodberry, R. D. (2012, May). *The Missionary Roots of Liberal Democracy*. Retrieved July 17, 2018, from https://www.academia.edu/2128659/The_Missionary_Roots_of_Liberal_Democracy